To Little Bro!

I hope that this first Jeep brings you fun and a smile.

Happy Christmas 2013

From

Nigel

WARTIME JEEPS

By Graham Scott
photography by Simon Clay

ACKNOWLEDGMENTS

I would like to thank, first and foremost, Fred Smith, whose collection of Jeeps is the finest in the world. The fact that his personally restored, private collection is "over here" in Britain is even more remarkable. Fred's enthusiasm, hands-on knowledge, wayward humour and generous assistance – not to mention the quiet but constant assistance of his partner Mo – helped make this book possible.

Paul Lincoln made both the Guards LRDG and the SAS elements possible – and my thanks to David Knudsen for the SAS vehicle. Paul's dedication to honouring the LRDG extended to him not shaving for several days before the photoshoot so as to add authenticity. Enthusiast and Jeep nut Mark Askew sold me books and gave freely of his specialist knowledge in equal measure. Stunt man Jim Dowdall let us play with his beloved Jeep in which he's done over 100,000 miles over the decades. Finally, my thanks go to the respected military historian Martin Windrow for his unfailing support and encyclopaedic knowledge.

Published 2011 by Herridge & Sons Ltd
Lower Forda, Shebbear
Beaworthy, Devon EX21 5SY, UK

© Copyright Graham Scott 2011

All rights reserved. No part of this publication may be reproduced in any form or by any means without the prior written permission of the publisher and the copyright holder.

ISBN 978-1-906133-37-5

Printed in China

CONTENTS

Introduction	4
Budd Pygmy	10
Bantam BRC-40	20
Willys MA	28
Ford GP Four Wheel Steer	36
Willys MB	46
Willys MB – Long Range Desert Group	56
Ford GPW	66
Ford GPA	78
Willys MT-TUG	92
Willys T-28 Half-Track	102
Willys MB – SAS	112
Appendix – Jeep specifications	120

INTRODUCTION

A Bantam chassis being tested at the factory. It managed to hold more than six times its specified 600lb rating.

Breaking news – this is a book about Jeeps. But in isolation they're just lumps of metal. These days increasingly either rusty lumps or gleaming and restored lumps but inanimate objects either way. What brings this story to life are the people involved. Those who worked around the clock to design and then build the Jeep. And of course those hundreds of thousands of service personnel who lived and sometimes died in their Jeep.

The irony is that, through those long years of people pouring their creativity and energy and sometimes lives into the Jeep, those vehicles remaining sometimes do seem to be more than simple inanimate objects and to have a character of their own.

But the legacy is more tangible than that. The Jeep was the answer to a problem that military planners had been struggling with for about half a century. There were numerous attempts made before it, but as soon as the first Jeep turned up for testing in 1940 it was obvious that, at last, and in one enormous effort, the answer was there, in the metal.

Again, the legacy goes further still. Here we are in the 21st century, and the effects of that first doorless, underpowered 4x4 are still in evidence on and off the road today. The entire 4x4 movement, the entire Sports Utility Vehicle market, is based absolutely on the original Jeep. It showed the way it could be done and, equally importantly, it worked, right out of the crate.

So how did it happen? Military planners had been working, ever since the internal combustion engine replaced the horse, to move troops and material more efficiently around the battlefield and also quickly between battlefields. Inevitably, the military were never given a clean sheet of paper, they always had to work with what was available and so, almost without exception, the early efforts were based on either cars, trucks or even tractors. Vehicles like the Ford Model T in America, the GAZ-61 in Russia and the Austin Seven in Britain all achieved some success but their limitations were obvious. Yet it was the diminutive little British car, the Austin Seven, which would be the link to the greatest 4x4 of them all.

The American Bantam Car Company produced Austin Seven-based vehicles and had the military interested in some for reconnaissance work. But the Americans hadn't really

INTRODUCTION

taken to this small car and by 1940 the company was heading towards the wall again after going bankrupt about ten years previously.

What they needed were more orders, and lots of them, if they were to survive. What they got was an invitation to tender for a new military vehicle.

On 27 June 1940 the American Quartermaster Corps Ordnance Technical Committee released the specifications for this vehicle, which were very specific. Among other things, they specified an empty weight of 1300lbs, four-wheel drive and a payload of 600lbs. While this was pretty demanding, it was nothing compared to the deadline to produce full blueprints, which was set for 22 July, less than a month later. And then, just ten weeks after the blueprints had to be delivered, any company competing had to produce 70 fully finished prototypes for testing.

It was a massive task and, given the deadlines, it would clearly be impossible to actually design and build everything from scratch. Things like engines and transmission would have to come off someone's shelf and the parts bins were obviously going to be raided. The question was, who would take up the challenge. The tender was sent to 135 companies but just one managed to come up with a complete set of blueprints by the deadline – Bantam.

Given that the tender was sent to some of the biggest vehicle manufacturers in America, how had this little Bantam managed to do it? The answer was by sheer graft, patriotic

The Bantam prototype outside the factory. Karl Probst is on the far left.

The Bantam prototype on an early test run around the factory with four aboard.

WARTIME JEEPS

The Bantam prototype being tested by the military at Camp Holabird.

determination, and by a mammoth, almost continuous session of two and a half days work by one man.

It must be remembered that this was June 1940, roughly 18 months before Pearl Harbor brought America into the Second World War. Across the Atlantic the German Blitzkrieg had smashed Europe's armies and taken the Wehrmacht and the Luftwaffe to the English Channel. While the Americans wrangled over a new military vehicle that didn't yet exist, every day young men were fighting and dying in the skies over England in what was becoming the Battle of Britain.

Although they were still living in peace, it was obvious to many American military planners that war was coming; they just didn't know when – yet when it did arrive they were still caught by surprise. But by the time the Japanese torpedo planes started sinking the US Pacific Fleet in December 1941, both the Willys MB and the Ford GPW were in production, and thousands of Jeeps had already been produced and delivered around the world.

This dramatic shift, from a list of requirements on a sheet of paper, to thousands upon thousands of vehicles in use within 18 months, is partly down to one man. Karl Probst was brought in to help Bantam meet the deadlines. The 56-year-old ran his own small engineering company in Detroit and had been persuaded to help by some heavy hitters in the military who knew the whole project was a huge demand for any company. With only about a week to go before the first deadline, Probst rolled up his sleeves, sat down with pen and paper and began to draw the blueprints for a new vehicle. He worked 18 hours, slept, worked another 18 hours straight and there it was – the Jeep.

The blueprints were thorough and realistic, and Bantam had suppliers like Spicer primed to deliver big ticket items like the axles, and they had a Continental engine giving a useful 46bhp. When the bidding started at the military's Camp Holabird on 22 July at 9am, the Bantam team was there, good to go. But they didn't quite have it all to themselves.

The Willys-Overland Company, like Bantam, was currently struggling, and behind it was a litany of takeovers, failures,

INTRODUCTION

busts and bad luck. It wasn't in as bad a situation as Bantam, and they still had enormous amounts of factory space, as well as a line of vehicles that were selling, but their future was looking rather bleak until this new project came along. Joseph Frazer had taken over as President the year before, a year after the new Vice President, Barney Roos. It was Roos who had recently overseen what would prove to be a critical project. He had taken their Whippet four-cylinder engine which had been in production since 1926 and managed to up power from 49bhp to 60bhp without in any way detracting from its usability and reliability. It was the Go-Devil engine.

Willys too had blueprints to put on the table alongside Bantam, plus they had much larger facilities and a strong engine. However, their blueprints were not as detailed or as complete as the Bantam ones and they were clearly unhappy about trying to meet the deadlines for prototypes. The contract went to Bantam, a contract worth over $170,000.

That should have been the start of a massive comeback by the David who'd taken on the Goliaths, but, as you'll read in the following chapters, life often isn't a story with a happy ending. What it did do was kickstart a process to which the military kept applying pressure over the coming year. More and more manufacturers became involved, the design was refined and refined until, by the time war really did break out for the Americans, they had the perfect tool for the job.

So what was it? The first consideration is that, while there are general and specific points that can be made about both the Willys MB and the Ford GPW, it must be remembered that they were made in dozens of factories scattered around America, fed by dozens of suppliers. Ford primarily made a vehicle to the Willys model, but over the long manufacturing run from 1941 to 1945 there were constant changes and upgrades. Sometimes these were planned improvements, sometimes there were simple shortages and panics and breakdowns which meant that unusual measures were taken.

For example, we know that in April 1943 the Willys had a change to the accelerator pedal and linkage to remove the rubber fitting, since rubber was becoming scarce and expensive. This detail was clearly a planned move, but at other times a Ford factory would use Willys-made engines for a while because of sudden demand and, specifically, Ford used Willys-built chassis from November 1943 to January 1944. But this wasn't because of an oversight, it was because the Ford body presses were being relocated to Willys' body contractor, American Central. That sign of the extraordinary way in which two normally competitive companies managed to work together for the common good is one of the many positives to come out of the Jeep story.

So, although it was in a state of constant flux, we can make a general description of what a Jeep was. In a manufacturing method copied for decades afterwards, the Jeep had a separate chassis with the body panels affixed to it. Two box-section side-members were joined by five cross-members, all fabricated from steel. The front cross-member was of a tubular cross-section on the Willys MB and of an inverted U section on the Ford GPW – these cross-members are visible below and behind the grilles and are one easy way to tell which is which.

Onto this chassis went the floor in 16-gauge low-carbon steel with 18-gauge body panels affixed. The engine under the bonnet was the Go-Devil engine, a 134cu in (2199cc) four-cylinder unit making 60bhp at 3600rpm. The generous cooling system contained 11 quarts of water, making it suitable for most environments.

The Borg & Beck clutch linked to a Warner transmission with three forward and one reverse gear, but with synchromesh only on second and third. The two-speed transfer case was made by Spicer and offered the ability to go at up to 55mph in top gear on the highway or else, by putting it into low ratio, drifting through mud or sand at just a few mph in second gear.

Spicer also supplied the axles. The vehicle featured four-wheel drive, with the front axle drive accessed via a lever to the driver's right, along with the main gear lever and the lever for the transfer case.

Suspension was leaf-sprung front and rear. It wasn't that compliant and was worse in the rear seat which was right over the rear axle. There were eight-leaf semi-elliptic springs in the front suspension and nine leaves in the rear. Damping was by telescopic shock absorbers, with various suppliers, including Bendix and Gabriel, supplying Willys or Ford.

Willys built two Quads, clearly based on the early Bantam prototype. It was Willys' more powerful Go-Devil engine that gave their design the edge.

WARTIME JEEPS

Jeeps roll off the Ford production line. Ford built nearly 280,000 GPW models.

Braking was by twin-shoe drums all round, hydraulically operated. A parking brake was also fitted.

Once full production was up and running, the Jeeps ran on Kelsey-Hayes split-rim combat wheels which had a run-flat capability, perfect for combat. These carried 6.00x16in tyres with non-directional tread so that nobody had to fiddle about working out which way the tread went; you could just bang them on and get going. The six-ply heavy duty tyres were made by a variety of manufacturers and carried inner tubes running normally at 30psi, depending on load and terrain.

Inside it was pretty spartan, with two metal frames for the front seats with squab cushions to base and back, and a bench seat in the rear with a squab seat and back. A canvas hood went over the whole thing and there were side panels that could be clipped and strapped into place, but they were seldom used as they restricted visibility too much. The windscreen was designed to fold flat for a better field of fire and also for when the vehicles were stacked for transportation.

Just simple nuts held the screen on either side so it could easily be removed. Because of this, there were no electrics for the wipers, which were just manually operated.

There were also really remarkably comprehensive spares and tool kits that went out with each vehicle. These included wrenches, fan belt, ball-peen hammer and even a roll of electrical tape.

Overall, the Jeep was 132ins long with an 80in wheelbase. Ground clearance under the axles was 8.7ins and 10ins under the bodywork. Height was 40ins over the bonnet, 70ins with the canvas roof up. A 15-gallon fuel tank sat under the driver's seat with consumption varying between about 13 and 27mpg, giving a range of about 200 miles if the driver took it easy.

You'll note that the one basic statistic missing from that list is the weight. You might recall that the original specifications called for a weight of 1300lbs. But we know that Karl Probst and Bantam thought this was simply unachievable and so ignored it. This led to other problems, like lower performance,

8

INTRODUCTION

The design process continued at the front. Jeeps were adapted in the field to do all sorts of jobs. A few months after D-Day, the British Royal Engineers were using this jeep on the Caen-Cherbourg railway line in Northern France.

higher fuel consumption, less load carrying and worse cross-country and hill-climbing performance. It was one of the reasons why the Bantam effort didn't really hit the big time.

The extra power of the Willys Go-Devil engine helped offset the weight and, to be fair to Bantam, nobody else could get the weight down to 1300lbs either. In the end that requirement was just ignored by everyone as unachievable without moving over to materials that were either unavailable in the quantities needed or would cost ridiculous amounts of money.

Remarkably, what with upgrades and additions, a normal Jeep coming off the line weighed in at not far off double the original limit, at 2450lbs and, by the end of the war, it was about 100lbs more than that. But it still worked, showing the basic rightness of the original design.

Of course, these are all figures for standard Jeeps, and it wasn't long before everyone realised that this most flexible of transports could be turned into just about anything. As you can see in these chapters, the Jeep could sprout two extra wheels, tracks, five machine guns and extra armour. There was even an amphibious version, the Seep.

And the power take-off turned a Jeep into a mobile powerhouse to run welders, cookers, searchlights, even a laundry. They could be converted to run on rails and towed goods carriages down the line everywhere from Europe to Australia and Burma. They towed bombers around airfields; their flat bonnet proved perfect for the padres to run religious services from (great for card games too), and while Jeeps took troops into combat, others were converted to ambulances and stretcher carrriers to bring the wounded out again.

So this is a book about the Jeep. People spent decades trying to come up with this vehicle. And people have spent the decades since enjoying the Jeep and all its successors and imitators all over the world. But this book is about the Jeep at war, the purpose for which it was solely designed. And this book is dedicated to those who created it, built it, drove it, lived in it, and fought in it.

Chapter 1
BUDD PYGMY

Have a look at the black and white photos on these pages. One of the Jeeps is marked "No 1 Jeep". There are many claimants to that title, but this particular Jeep certainly has a claim, with photographic back-up.

What you see is a three-dimensional manifestation of the exact drawings which Bantam had made. When Bantam's initial prototype was on test at Camp Holabird – as you can read in the next chapter – not only the Army and Bantam were present at the tests, but also competitors from Ford and Willys-Overland. The Army was concerned at Bantam's apparent lack of industrial strength and took the position that it now owned all the blueprints. So, to cover all the bases, the Army simply copied the Bantam blueprints and gave them to both Ford and Willys.

This decision meant that both Ford and Willys were able to produce their own prototypes quickly, although it was also at their own expense. As a result, Willys delivered its prototype, called the Quad, to Camp Holabird on 11 November 1940 and the Ford prototype, the Pygmy, arrived 12 days later.

But Ford wanted to produce two prototypes and, since they didn't have the capability of doing so in the short timeframe, they farmed the build of a second vehicle out to one of their suppliers, based on a chassis provided by Ford. The Edward G Budd Manufacturing Company is one of the unsung heroes of vehicle development since Edward Gowen Budd was the first man to mass produce all-steel vehicle frames to replace clumsy assemblies of wood, steel and paint. His company already built the half-ton Dodge Command Car.

The company was also a major manufacturer of rail rolling stock as well as a supplier of pressed steel panels and so was a highly suitable supplier for the second Pygmy. This particular vehicle, the original Budd prototype, was believed to have been destroyed at some point, but it was found, rotting but largely intact, in a scrapyard in the Californian desert. If it had disappeared we would probably have thought highly of it and assumed it was identical to the Ford Pygmy. But it isn't.

Instead it is testament to what happens when everyone is working against virtually impossible deadlines and there isn't the time to go through things carefully. Clearly, the original blueprints weren't quite right in a few areas, and the Ford Pygmy shows that the discrepancies were noted before the vehicle was finished, and they were duly fixed. Not so in the Budd. The American Quartermaster Corps (QMC) had had a hand in drawing up the blueprints given to the other competitors and there's no doubt that not enough time was spent on the bodywork design.

In fact, it was Clarence Kramer, who was Ford's Design Engineer, who took it upon himself to make improvements to the original drawing when he produced the Ford Pygmy. Both Ford and Budd were basing their build on two identical chassis which Ford had managed to build in just a month. Ford elected to put forward not only the Kramer-designed machine, but also the Budd-built machine, which was indeed to the original specifications, for the test. Both the Budd and the Ford were delivered at the same time, on November 23, even arriving on the same train from Detroit to Holabird.

From a distance the Budd looks fine, but the problems start when you try to actually sit in the thing. The thought instantly occurs that someone took the name just a little too seriously. There's no door, but the space between the seat and steering wheel is so tight that it's really difficult to get in, certainly impossible for a laden soldier in a hurry. To make matters worse, the floor is just a clutter of levers. Levers for the main gearbox, the two-speed transfer case and the front axle drive, not forgetting the handbrake.

And once in you can't see where you're going. Unless indeed

A photo taken at Ford's Dearborn airfield in 1941 shows this extensive line of Jeeps. If you look along the line, just behind the car and men in the foreground you can see the Budd – the driver is the only one wearing a hat. Just above the car you can see the headlights sticking up above the bonnet line, unlike all the others. The "No 1 Jeep" stencil can just be made out on the bodywork.

you are a pygmy, the top of the windscreen frame is right in your line of vision. It's a thick frame too, with massive side supports which don't owe a lot to car manufacture.

Some elements are pure Budd, like the grab handles on the exterior. They're huge and almost certainly come off a train, not a car. And, if we're still viewing this in a rather negative light, things don't improve much under the bonnet, although the blame for that lies squarely with Ford rather than Budd.

At this point Ford didn't have a really suitable four-cylinder car engine to shoehorn in, but what they did have was the engine from the Ford 9N tractor. The 9N four-cylinder engine produced lots of torque and an adequate power output of 45bhp at 3600rpm. But a tractor engine is designed to run all day at low revs, it's not designed for rapid and constant changes of engine speed and load. To compound the problem, the engine was mated to an old Model A transmission with three forward and one reverse gear. To make the engine more lively, they'd taken off the governor, but this simply meant the engine ran its bearings, while trying to make it work through an elderly transmission with no synchromesh showed how unsuitable this powerplant was.

Above the engine was a slightly rounded bonnet with a central knurled knob, a complex item that would need to be simplified for mass production. If you look at later Jeeps in this book you can clearly see how the whole "sit up and beg" stance has been slightly modified, but this is still the base look of all Jeeps.

Naturally things changed on all later vehicles, some of them because it dawned on designers that they were making a vehicle for soldiers, not for nice fathers and their families. On the Budd there's an ignition key and steering lock on the steering column but it didn't take long before soldiers started wandering off with the keys, rendering the vehicles immobile. That posed more of a risk than having the vehicle stolen, so later models were stripped of all unnecessary or questionable items, like ignition keys.

Overall the Budd is a very strong vehicle, ironically helped by Budd's experience at building trains. For example the spare wheel on the rear panel has massive support under it. This was stripped back on later models, as you'll see later in this book, but this then put too much strain on the rear panel so that, eventually, more reinforcing had to be re-introduced.

But, strong or not, and impressive as it was that Ford managed to get not only its own prototype to Camp Holabird but also the Budd version, it was all in vain. The military looked at the two vehicles and chose to test only the Ford Pygmy, leaving the Budd out of the testing. That seems like a sensible decision when you see the reality of how awkward the Budd Pygmy was to get in and out of and to drive. At least the Ford version had taken account of issues in the blueprints.

Later the Budd prototype was used for War Bond and fundraising drives in the USA before, apparently, disappearing for ever. Seventy years later, here it is, complete with "No 1 Jeep" stencil. Given this is the most exact version of those original blueprints, that stencil is well deserved.

WARTIME JEEPS

This is so obviously the Jeep outline yet the eye catches those details that mark it out as a prototype. Early Willys models like the Quad came with a single glass in the windscreen, but the Ford-designed Budd had this two-pane design, which proved stronger and easier to fix than one large piece of glass.

The headlight guard demonstrates the sheer strength of this particular model. It forms an integral part of the mudguard and the front grille. The front grille itself looks strong enough to be a cattle grid. Note the blackout light to the left, which on later models was mounted directly on the mudguard.
The Pygmy, the Ford-built entry that went for testing alongside this vehicle, had the headlights inside the grille behind strong guards. That was a far better solution than this, and was copied on all subsequent mass-production models

12

Strength is good, but over-engineering leads to excessive weight. The size of the windscreen surround would be more suited to a truck, not to a light reconnaissance vehicle. Note the pivot point for unscrewing to lay the windscreen flat on the bonnet. This is far further back than it was on all subsequent models, and is a more complex, heavy and therefore expensive assembly that doesn't belong on a mass-production vehicle. In contrast, the wing mirror has no adjustment on the stalk length, a refinement needed to cater for such a wide range of drivers.

The "No 1 Jeep" stencil is authentic and documented. Note the sheer size of the handles on the exterior, more than man enough to be used to heave the Jeep out of a ditch.

WARTIME JEEPS

The spare wheel moved around between different models and was invariably offset instead of in the middle, as here. In keeping with their strong engineering traits, Budd gave substantial and heavy support to the rear wheel and bumper assembly. Future efforts at lightening this support led to the rear sections cracking, which then had to be reinforced again.

Detail at the top of the windscreen showing one of the manual windscreen wipers. A lever the other side of the screen could be moved back and forward to activate the two small blades. Note also the popper stops for the canvas hood which would have snapped into place along the top of this substantial screen frame.
The glass in the screen could be actually swung out a bit to allow more air through. The complex hinge is inside the two large circular bits of the upright at either end of the top of the screen. You can see the large screw with wings just behind the one to the left of this picture which would help lock the glass into place. This mechanism, sort of like a giant cat flap, was heavily over-engineered.

BUDD PYGMY

The engine bay shows how the Ford 9N tractor engine sits quite far back in the bay, making access to the rear of the engine and the fourth plug quite difficult. The battery to the right is clearly not the correct electricity source, which would have been two six-volt batteries sitting where the current battery is positioned. Note the oil-bath air cleaner to the left rear. Note also the two forked grips at the very top of the picture – they only appear on this vehicle and their purpose is unclear.

The 9N engine had its provenance stamped into the top of the cylinder head. The heads were always this grey colour.

15

WARTIME JEEPS

View looking down from the passenger side of the engine bay. The main issue here is that the exhaust manifold is at the top, nearest to the camera. This meant that, to access the carburettor, you had to get past the hot manifold and access was severely restricted. While this situation was improved on the Ford GP, this engine had more fundamental problems to overcome.

Rear axle looking forward. At this stage there were the leaf springs but not yet the telescopic shock absorbers that followed for mass production. Instead there were these Houdaille dampers later found on the 6x6 model – see Chapter 9. This basic set up would remain effectively the same throughout the Jeep's long history. This is the Spicer axle with 4.88:1 ring and pinions.

BUDD PYGMY

One of the major drawbacks of the Budd was the sheer difficulty of getting in. That distinctive double-scallop body shape looks graceful but ensures no soldier could get in or out in a hurry.

Shot clearly showing the strange combination of flat grille but rounded bonnet. The knurled knob on the front was unscrewed to release up the bonnet. The headlights started off on top of the huge mudguards, as with this model, but were simply too obtrusive. From here they moved in stages to half into sculpted mudguards and then into the main grille on later models, more out of harm's way.

WARTIME JEEPS

The dash gives a period feel more than the rest of the vehicle. Note the hand throttle (the T knob top right). Although it looks more dated than later production fascias, the dash does feature the same basic five sets of information and even has speed ranges for the gears on the speedo.

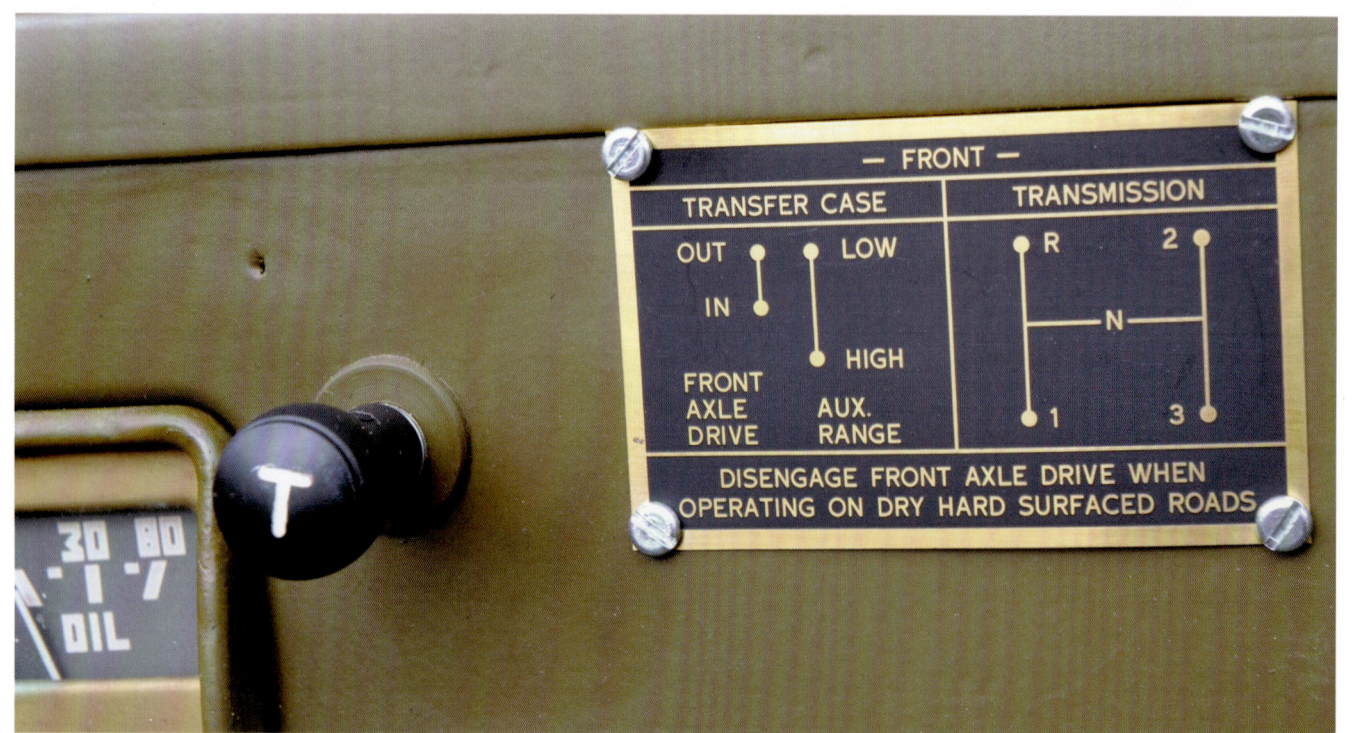

Clear instructions for the driver, to the right of the dials and the hand throttle. The sign shows the concern that soldiers would try to drive on a hard surface with the front diff locked, which could cause serious transmission and steering problems.

18

BUDD PYGMY

Spartan interior didn't change fundamentally throughout the long runs of subsequent models. Note how the double scallop of the bodyshape is echoed by the high seat sides – fortunately two problems which never made it into production. Similarly, the four levers on the floor were reduced to three when the handbrake was moved to the fascia. This view clearly shows the fuel tank under the driver's seat, where it stayed throughout although it did gain in size.

The three pedals, with the brake pedal partially obscured. Note the ignition and steering lock just visible on the steering column which was dropped from later vehicles as crewmen tended to wander off with the keys.

Chapter 2
BANTAM BRC-40

Someone described as a bantam is small and feisty – and that certainly described the American Bantam Car Company. It was also a company in dire financial straits and, by the summer of 1940, it was struggling for survival.

American Bantam was one of the 135 companies that received the specifications on 27 June from the American Quartermaster Corps Ordinance Technical Committee. And it was the only one of the 135 to present full blueprints when bidding opened for the near $175,000 contract on 22 July at 9am.

As you can read in the Introduction, this was a triumph of David and Goliath proportions. The only other company to offer any drawings were Willys-Overland and theirs were not in anything like the same state of completeness. They also tried to extend the deadline for the prototype, which stood at just 49 days away.

Unsurprisingly the contract went to Bantam, showing that

A Bantam BRC-40 belonging to the British 6th Armoured Division with complex machine-gun mount and extra storage bins

the early bird really does get the worm. Now they had to produce a prototype in a hurry and there was no way to do that other than to raid the parts bins of stuff they already had. Nevertheless, the design showed the basic "rightness" of the Jeep concept as drawn by Bantam's Karl Probst.

The steel ladder-frame chassis had utilitarian, doorless steel body panels fitted, with high mudguards which exposed the wheels, leaf springs and telescopic shock absorbers. Unlike later versions of the Jeep and indeed of the BRC-40, this prototype had a rounded front end that owed itself to car design rather than military. The Budd/Ford prototype on the previous pages is actually more what the original Bantam looked like than the fractionally later one you see here.

Just about all of the rest of the vehicle came from elsewhere. Under the rounded bonnet was a 46hp Continental four-cylinder engine feeding through a Warner Gear three-speed gearbox with reverse. The two-speed transfer case was from Spicer, who also supplied the Studebaker axles. But this vehicle was more than just a box of bits and, when it was delivered for testing, on schedule, on 23 September 1940 it immediately impressed.

Testing spread over three weeks and over 3000 miles at the Camp Holabird military facility. Testing was brutal, as it needed to be if it was to simulate both war and the heavy-handed habits of soldiers, but the Bantam passed with flying colours. The company at once set about producing the 70 examples that were called for by its successful bid. But Bantam was a featherweight in terms of mass production and other heavy hitters were massing.

Both Ford and Willy-Overland had people on hand when that first Bantam was being tested. As discussed in the previous chapter, their frantic note-taking was unnecessary as the

BANTAM BRC-40

Army simply handed them copies of the Bantam blueprints.

Not only was the Army uneasy about Bantam's ability to ramp up production if needed, but they were also concerned about the vehicle's weight, height and power. On the specifications, weight had been stipulated at a maximum of 1300 pounds but Probst was certain that was impossible and had simply ignored it. As a result the Bantam was about 600lbs overweight, which had an effect on performance and practicality.

Things were helped by an enormous cavalry officer managing to lift the Bantam out of a small ditch on his own, so it was decided to up the weight limit anyway. However, as you can read in the Introduction, none of the others could meet the 1300lbs requirement so it was a practical solution to simply allow heavier vehicles.

When both Ford and Willys produced their first prototypes they looked remarkably like the Bantam – given they'd been working off the blueprints that's hardly a big surprise. As they faced up to a revised Bantam in back-to-back tests in November 1940, it was against a background of Bantam having secured the first contract for 1500 vehicles already. But ahead lay much bigger production prizes.

Constant revisions by all three manufacturers led to the Service Test finals, and it soon became clear that the Willys was better than the offerings from Ford or Bantam. With the huge contracts going to Willys and then Ford, Bantam was left out on a limb. They copied the square front of the Ford GP, which they incorporated into the BRC-40, and eventually they produced over 2600 vehicles. (By the way, BRC-40 stands for Bantam Reconnaissance Command – 40 horsepower.) Compared to the hundreds of thousands produced by the two companies who had literally stood on the sidelines while they watched the BRC-40 on test, this was a bitter blow for Bantam.

They had created the Jeep, or the first incarnation of it, and they'd hit every deadline, unlike anyone else. Their unique blueprints had been taken from them and given to their competitors, but still they'd behaved impeccably – their military sales representative, retired Navy Commander Charles Payne, promised that Bantam would share technical data and fully co-operate with the other manufacturers if Bantam couldn't manage the large-scale production that seemed likely.

Yet it was Bantam that spent the rest of the war making torpedoes, aircraft landing gear and vehicle trailers. After the end of the war Bantam went bust.

This view shows the square-set lines of the BRC-40, with flat panels, and squarer corners than the later Jeeps. Note also the three bonnet hinges, visible on the exterior, even though the bonnet isn't especially heavy. This is obviously not a fully production-finished vehicle, and nor was it especially meant to be (note things like the extra little fiddly metal sheet guides at the base of the windscreen), and yet so much of it is quintessentially Jeep. It seems a shame that only about 2600 were ever made and that the company that came up with the idea never got to reap the rewards.

WARTIME JEEPS

The BRC-40's floorpan features a simpler single curve down in front of the rear bench seat, instead of the more complex curvatures of the Budd. It is also simpler and less of an obstacle around the main gearlever. The seats too feature simpler sides so as to offer some support but not obstruct entry and exit.

Compared to the Ford-penned Budd design, the windscreen frame is considerably lighter but quite sturdy enough. Note, near the hinge, the nut and bolt that offer some fine-tuning for the exact angle that the windscreen stands at. Note also that the Bantam did not have a glovebox in this version.

BANTAM BRC-40

Everyone took a different direction on how best to accommodate the headlights. Ford clearly got it right first time with the Pygmy and simply incorporated them into the front end, in front of the radiator and behind the front grille. Willys, with both the Quad and the MA (see later chapter) still had the headlights on top of the wings as did the Budd in the previous chapter. Bantam took a halfway position and put them into scallops in the front of the mudguards. This made a nice scoop for mud and water and was complex to build. Note that a precautionary strengthening bar connects the bottom of the mudguard with the bodywork.

Another view of the whole front wing, showing how this design led to more complexity, weight and hence cost. Designing the headlights into the front grille fixed virtually all these problems. Note the rubber stop, one of three on the bonnet for when the bonnet was raised or the windscreen lowered. War shortages meant that pure rubber stops never went into mass production.

WARTIME JEEPS

The original Bantam had a rounded front end, but by the time of the BRC-40 this had been changed into the flat grille look of the Ford offerings. This shot shows how low the bonnet was on the BRC-40, lower than its successors, but, then, it did not have the Go-Devil engine underneath. Although Bantam was first out of the blocks and created the look that became that of the Jeep, this BRC-40 owes some of its appearance to its competitors. Although they started it, Bantam certainly didn't finish it.

On the original Bantam prototype tested, the spare wheel had been at the rear on the driver's side. By the time of the BRC-40 the wheel, and its attendant weight, had moved over to the other side. This was in line with both Ford and Willys, who both had the engine positioned slightly left of centre. This movement have gone some way to balancing that out, but, as we will see, further steps were needed.

BANTAM BRC-40

The floorpan of the BRC-40 was quite different from the others, as you can see with the ribbing evident here. The bumperettes, either side of the towing hitch, are relatively lightweight and offer no support to the spare wheel carrier. Note also the exhaust, which exits over the rear axle and is aimed to the rear. Although the Bantam already had telescopic shock absorbers, it's noticeable how far they are angled from the line of axle movement, which isn't ideal for maximum damper performance.

The much simpler lines of the Bantam ensured that it was considerably easier to jump in and out of compared to the Ford/Budd. At this stage the Bantam still offered very upright, right-angled mudguards compared to the more flowing lines of the later Ford and Willys models. The vehicle has a slight forward angled stance rather than the flat balance of later vehicles, giving more space under the rear wheelarches than was really necessary.

WARTIME JEEPS

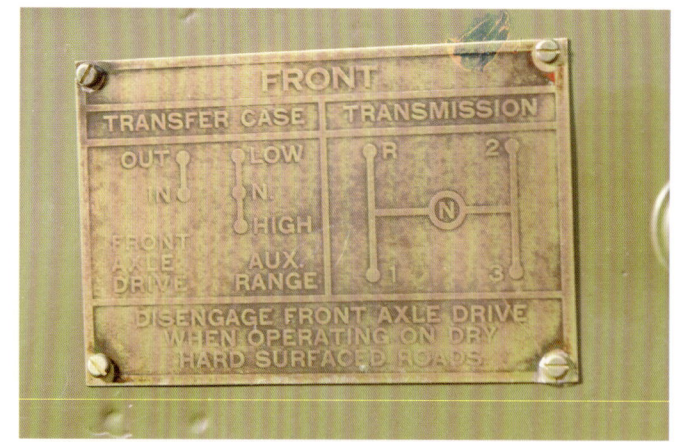

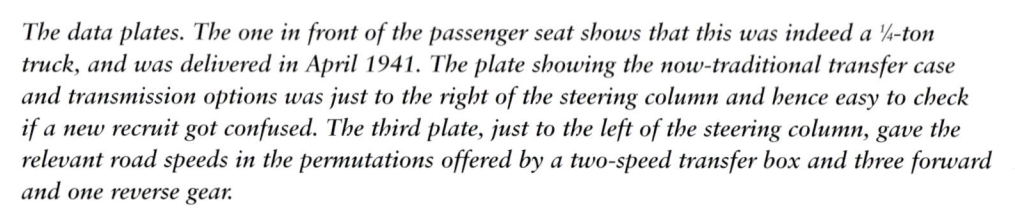

The data plates. The one in front of the passenger seat shows that this was indeed a ¼-ton truck, and was delivered in April 1941. The plate showing the now-traditional transfer case and transmission options was just to the right of the steering column and hence easy to check if a new recruit got confused. The third plate, just to the left of the steering column, gave the relevant road speeds in the permutations offered by a two-speed transfer box and three forward and one reverse gear.

To the left of the speedo, and in easy view, this single dial offered information on the four essential elements of water temperature, fuel level, oil pressure and battery charge rate. The instruments came from other cars in the Bantam range.

BANTAM BRC-40

The engine bay in the Bantam, looking rather different from the others in the book. The structure is reinforced at the bulkhead by two metal sheets bolted into place on either wing. You can see the massive air filter, which has the carburettor below it and then the exhaust manifold below that. The Continental four-cylinder engine may not have been perfect, but it was a big step up from the tractor engine of the Ford competition. (Obviously, the modern battery is not correct.) In fact, driven today, this feels like a perky engine and doesn't seem to give away as much as you might imagine to the much more powerful Go-Devil engine – at least, not until you start pushing it like a Camp Holabird tester.

The rear bench seat could be folded up flat against the back panel. You can see how the back section can slide down the two square tubes as the base section hinges up from the rear. Note the lockable cargo boxes on either side, which could hold smaller items of kit away from loose fingers. This is also a good view showing the rear of the spare wheel holder, to which the spare wheel was attached with three bolts.

27

Chapter 3

WILLYS MA

They say competition improves the breed, and here's living proof. The Willys-Overland Quad which went up against the Ford Pygmy (almost identical to the Budd version in Chapter 1) was a big, heavy vehicle with a complex rounded front, even more rounded than the Pygmy. Like every other entrant, it was too heavy, but it did have an ace – the Go-Devil engine.

More powerful than any of the competition, this engine was enough to get Willys into the Service Test finals, a further and final round of tests that took place between Bantam, Ford and Willys. Willys already had an order for 1500 units, but the order made clear that this was for a vehicle superior to the Quad. With the revised weight limit set at 2160lbs, the Willys still broke the scales at 2423lbs, the heaviest of the three. There was nothing for it: Willys was going to have to go through the vehicle component by component to lose a lot of weight.

Decades before computer programming could have done the heavy lifting, this was a huge task, undertaken by Barney Roos. The attention to detail meant reducing the layers of paint to one coat – that saved 9lbs. A new seat design saved 18lbs and every bolt and washer was reviewed. The big number came from replacing the heavy carbon steel frame with one in lower gauge, higher grade steel, which alone saved 115lbs.

The complex and heavy front end went, replaced by a flat bonnet and grille with the letters "Willys" stamped into the bonnet front above the grille. Behind that grille the Go-Devil engine remained largely unchanged since it was a clear vote-winner.

This model, known as the MA, was the first definitive Jeep. It won the final "US Tentative Specifications USA-LP-997A", won an initial order for 16,000 revised models and set in train an enormous and unprecedented building programme across both the Willys and Ford industrial empires.

So, here it is, the Jeep. In many ways it changed little from here on in, although the main difference is the visible one of the headlamps still being set up above the wings, instead of being set into the front grille. The grille itself is made of individual iron bars welded top and bottom, a system replaced by a stamped assembly when the really big numbers started being produced.

Behind the grille is the famous Go-Devil engine, a four-cylinder unit that dated back to 1926. When it was already 12 years old, it was uprated to go into the Willys Whippet so by the time of World War II it was actually quite an elderly engine which had been breathed on for more power several times. This should have resulted in a fragile, over-stressed engine, but the 2199cc unit was a paragon of power and durability.

With 60bhp at 4000rpm and 105lb ft of torque at a lowly 2000rpm, it could go on for, as we know, nearly three quarters of a century and counting. One of the reasons for this durability was the rather oversized cooling system. This ran 11 quarts of water and helped the Jeeps keep going even in the close confines of the jungle, and when pulling ridiculous loads through deep mud. Of course, to weary, grubby soldiers, this was also a copious source of hot water for shaving, cooking and, occasionally, washing.

The engine ran through a Borg & Beck clutch to the Warner transmission with a Spicer two-speed transfer box. Back in the days before sequential, paddle-controlled gearboxes, the average soldier had to get used to a gearbox with three forward speeds and one reverse, but with synchromesh only on second and third.

Inside, the main difference from later models is that most of the controls and levers are on the dashboard. On the floor are two levers, for two-speed transmission and for front axle lock, while the gearshift moved up to the steering column and the umbrella handbrake moved to the left of the dashboard. Compared to, say, the Ford Pygmy, it's a model of simplicity and easy to control as well as get in and out – although the column shift is fairly easy to get wrong and isn't as definite as the floor-mounted unit.

Maintaining the theme of simplicity, inside there are three rather than the later five dials, with a speedometer (on the right) balanced by a combination gauge for amps, oil and fuel. The third dial between them is a temperature gauge.

This particular model has been a working vehicle for 70 years – so far – and is fully road legal, so ignore the more modern additions, like the graphics and the indicators. At the risk of sounding anthropomorphic, simply being in the presence of this Jeep tells you it's also been in action.

Most of the MAs went out on the Arctic convoys to Russia as part of the Lend-Lease programme. And most of these disappeared into the great charnel house of the Eastern Front, but the odd example, like this one, somehow survived and came back to the West. It's impossible to describe, but there's an air of rugged toughness to this vehicle that is missing from prototypes and one-offs that we know went for testing but not into the combat zone. It's a workhorse, like all Jeeps, but this one is a warhorse too.

Fairly crude, but amazingly effective. An axle twister shows off the Jeep's agility, with both axles working to keep all four wheels on the ground and therefore capable of driving forward. This shot shows that the front mudguards were still rather over-represented, something that would be cut back on later models. Note also the single windscreen wiper, operated by hand on the inside of the screen. Twin wipers, operated by hand again but with a bar connecting the two wipers, weren't introduced until the MB model in the summer of 1943.

WARTIME JEEPS

Great view of the blunt end of the Willys – as opposed to the other end which is also blunt. Note the Willys name stamped into the front of the bonnet. You can clearly see that the grille is made up of individual bars, a laborious procedure and a heavy result. The headlights are still up above the front mudguards, which at this stage are substantial items with curved front panels for support rather than a simple metal brace as on the Budd. Note the single bonnet stop, which has already lost all rubber content. This shot clearly shows one easy way to tell a Willys and a Ford apart, once the front ends became more similar on later models. The front crossmember is of a tubular design and performs a small arch on the Willys but is of U-shaped steel on the Ford.

The bonnet was held down by spring-loaded catches bolted onto grille uprights. The sprung bonnet catches moved from being on the front of the grille, as here, to the sides, behind the headlights, on later models.
Note how the stone guard around the headlight is incorporated into the grille and bumper design for extra strength. Next to it is the blackout light and next to that is a modern indicator, reminding us that these adaptable vehicles can still be made easily road-legal all these decades later.

30

WILLYS MA

Made in America, shipped to Russia where it saw combat, then shipped back decades later to the heart of England via Holland. Note how the front mudguard shape has already started to round off the square look of the Bantam. The exhaust is clearly seen here, exiting on the left. At this stage it had a round silencer but around May 1942 it was changed to an oval shape.

Simple windscreen hinge was easy to operate and made it fast to put the screen up or down. Compare this to the Budd to see how cheap and easy this solution is. The wing mirror, not something soldiers use a lot, has several adjustment points, by contrast. It would take only seconds for the windscreen to be completely removed, aided by there being no electrical connections since the wipers were manually operated.

WARTIME JEEPS

The umbrella-type handbrake is visible on the left of the dashboard. On subsequent models this was moved to the middle to give someone other than the driver a fighting chance of stopping the vehicle if it all went wrong. The gearlever moved from the floor to the steering column and is easy to get at although not as easy to use as the floor-mounted option. Opposite the gearlever on the column is a much later indicator assembly that is obviously a retro-fit. Above the handbrake, one of the two catches that helped hold the windscreen in place. The pedals have progressed from being glorified buttons to the sort of pedals we'd expect to see today. The floor is relatively uncluttered with just the transfer case and front diff lock levers on the floor ahead of the seats. The steering wheel was made of a type of green rubber but, starting in September 1942, this was changed to a composite wheel to save rubber for more valuable uses.

Excellent shot showing the kind of axle articulation possible without a wheel leaving the ground. Note how the leaf springs and their hangers, along with the shock absorber, are now at full stretch. On the other side they're at full compression, up inside the wheelarch. Compare the location and effectiveness of these shock absorbers compared to the angles demanded of the Bantam in the previous chapter. They're clearly pulling in much more of a straight line and are therefore more effective.

WILLYS MA

Ignore the modern accoutrements like the lights and indicators. This is a good view of the spare wheel holder, again over on the passenger side of the vehicle. With three bolt holes it worked well but overall the heavy wheel has less support than on, say, the Budd. The blackout lights above the modern indicators still have rubber trim surrounds, another luxury that had to go soon after Pearl Harbor.

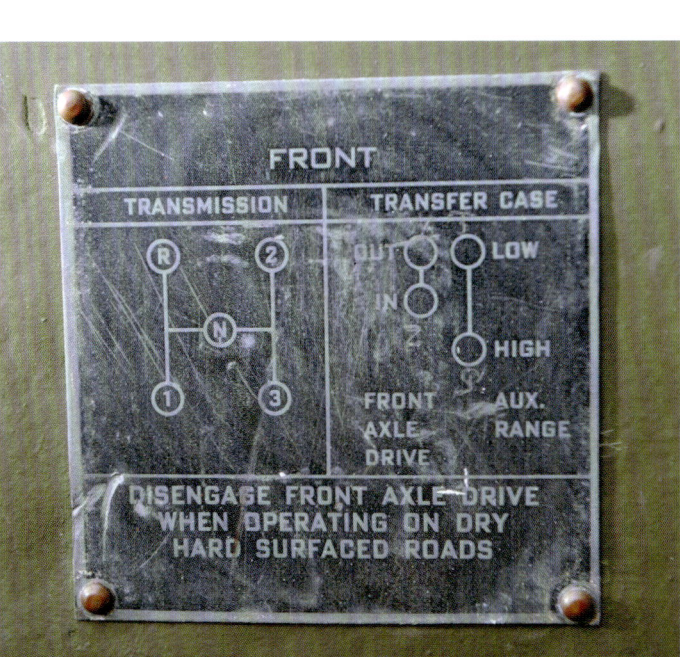

The three plates that we'd expect by now. The vehicle was delivered on 14 July 1941. The three plates sit in a line in front of the passenger, as there was no glovebox.

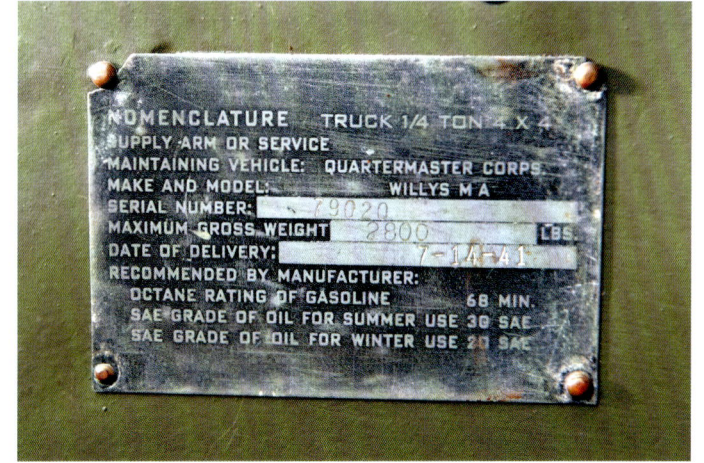

WARTIME JEEPS

This is actually a Willys MB engine rather than the MA although they're not wildly different. The air cleaner is original MA, leading over to the carb on the right.

Fine view of the seating components. Originally this would have been filled with rubber, but as that became scarce animal hair and rubber and then animal hair and springs took their place. The outer material was heavyweight cotton duck that was both fire-resistant and waterproof.

The simple three-dial display to the right of the driver. Fuel, oil and amps are covered by the dial on the left, with the temperature gauge in the middle and a speedo and mileometer on the right. Rather stylish dials for a military vehicle.

WILLYS MA

Although the seating material looks rather bright – it's clearly a replica rather than original – it is made to original specifications and colour. To the left of the image you can see the small handle that the driver had to find a hand for if he wanted to make the windscreen wiper work – while he steered, changed gear and wondered if that dark shape was friend or foe. The two stowage bins each side of the rear seat were considerably larger on the MA and could hold a reasonable amount of kit away from the elements.

Spicer axles, shock absorbers often made by Monroe, leaf springs and good ground clearance. Note the robust spring hangers at the top of the shot and the gearbox guard further forward. Compared to a modern 4x4 this is amazingly simple and wouldn't offer the same ride quality – but it is still running reliably more than half a century later, having survived World War Two.

Chapter 4

FORD GP FOUR WHEEL STEER

In the same way that the Service Test finals galvanised Willys-Overland into building the MA model, so they pushed Ford into producing the GP. Whether those two letters were the basis of the name Jeep is debatable, but they don't stand for General Purpose, as often supposed. G stood for Government since it was a government contract they were after and P denoted the company's 80in wheelbase reconnaissance car.

Whatever it was called, the GP was an improvement on the Pygmy. At a stroke, the designers came up with the definitive bonnet shape that would remain for the rest of the war to come and which would be integrated into the design no matter who built it. At this stage Ford started what would be a bit of a fetish for them, which was marking parts with the Ford logo. As you'll see later in the book, this spread to just about every item large or small, but for now you can clearly see the Ford script embossed into the rear panel by the spare wheel.

Ford was still dragging its corporate feet slightly as it was focusing on passenger cars and also had some labour problems, but the scale of the orders that might be in the offing was beginning to concentrate the management's minds. However, no amount of focus could magically produce a new engine so under that new bonnet was the same tractor engine as in the Pygmy (and Budd, see previous chapter).

However, some practical changes had been made. In the Pygmy the carburettor was right at the bottom, below the manifold, which would have made servicing and access a nightmare. On the GP the Holley carburettor was raised to the top, above the exhaust manifold. Even so, it's noticeable how far back the engine sits in the engine bay, so access to the rear spark plug was difficult. Given the reliability of this engine in this application, that spelled further trouble.

Of course, the obvious stand-out for the particular model photographed here is the four-wheel steering to go with the four-wheel drive. The US cavalry wanted this option as they figured it would increase manoeuvrability on reconnaissance missions. Indeed, Bantam had build eight four-wheel steer models but they were simply cobbled together with the front and rear axles steering in different directions. This made for a terrific turning circle but it also made handling distinctly odd, notably at speed.

The Ford answer was to use a Spicer axle facing the front in the front and another facing the rear in the rear, with tie rods connecting the steering to both axles independently and at different ratios. The effect was that if the driver fed in minimal steering inputs, as he would when driving at speed on the open road, only the front wheels steered so it behaved like a normal Jeep. After quarter of a turn of steering the rear unit came into play in a progressive way so that the more steering input, the greater the activation of the rear steering.

The cavalry approved and there is no doubt that in certain situations the ability to get the hell out of there, especially if it means turning round on a narrow road and getting away, would have been a life saver.

Trials of this vehicle went on in the autumn of 1941, with the last of them being delivered for test in October of that year. At this point Ford had already won a contract to produce 1500 standard GP models and negotiations were going on to ascertain whether just Willys, or both Willys and Ford would start producing vast numbers of Jeeps. While these discussions took place, the military placed more orders for the Ford GP with 4456 eventually being produced. As with the Willys MA, many of these went for Lend-Lease and so disappeared into Russia, never to be seen again.

The fate of the four-wheel steer Ford GPs was sealed in March 1942. While the cavalry wanted them, those in the military charged with costings and commonality of parts simply couldn't justify them. Not only were they more expensive to make, but they also meant that items that were in relatively short supply, like the Spicer axles, would suddenly be needed in double the quantities for the four-wheel steer versions. The huge production lines at Ford's factories would soon be churning out Ford GPWs in massive quantities, and nothing was going to be allowed to slow that juggernaut down.

Looking on the bright side, the other battle which had been going on was a campaign between many in the military and those who might be said to have had a vested interest. By the time of the awarding of the contract for an initial 16,000 vehicles, a contract which went to Willys, Ford had begun a vigorous campaign to win the battle for production. It had a lot of supporters, right up to the highest levels of The Quartermaster Corps, the military and even politics, and for a while it looked like the Ford GP, with its tractor engine, was going to be the standard Jeep produced for the war.

But the War Production Office took an objective view, helped by its head being William Knudsen, a Dane who had already seen his country occupied by the Germans. Despite Ford's lobbying, the contract (as described in the previous chapter) went to Willys. As we will see in Chapter 6, this was far from the end for Ford, as the future held enormous volumes of vehicles for both Ford and Willys. And, from the soldier's point of view, they were all making the right vehicle.

The generic Jeep shape has moved on further with the Ford GP. Specifically, the headlights and blackout lights have been refined in their position inside the grille, where they were on the original Pygmy. This in turn means that the mudguards don't have to be so substantial and have accordingly been reduced in size and weight. The bonnet is also light, simple to produce and perfectly matches the front end. This was the standard look until the grille was replaced by a stamped grille, but all Ford GPs featured this grille.

WARTIME JEEPS

Doesn't it look strange? The way the steering worked, you could only get this extreme amount of "opposite lock" into the back wheels at very low speed – the prospect of it being able to do this at high speed is not a pleasant one. Ford had a significant advantage here, as their four-wheel steering was more advanced than the others. However, the additional complication, weight and expense – not to mention using up valuable resources like steering boxes at double the rate – meant that the cavalry had to ride into the sunset without them.

FORD GP

To the right of this shot you can see the back of the transfer case with the propshaft taking power to the rear axle on the left. On the far side you can just see a tubular steering arm coming back from the front steering box, underneath the driver. This then connects with the second steering box – the round device bolted to the far chassis rail – from which proportional steering movements are made by the final steering arm to the rear wheels. A good shot showing the chassis rails, transmission and the front attachment points for the rear springs. The exhaust silencer box is at the very top right of the shot, exiting to the passenger side.

The view from the other side, with the front wheels on the left. In the middle is the grey sump of the engine. On the far side of the chassis rail you can see the take-off for the second steering arm going towards the rear.

The 9N engine was still the only unit Ford could use, despite its definite unsuitability. Note how far back the engine still sits, giving difficult access to the rear cylinder. This is the same engine as in the Budd, but it has been slightly improved. The carburettor is now up high – back left – so it is above the manifold and easier to access. The distributor has also been moved upwards, away from water and mud – just to the right of the large air cleaner.

On the rear bulkhead, just to the right of the block, is the black shape of the coil. This was known colloquially as "the five minute coil", since this Ford-made item was reckoned to have a life expectancy of about that!
At the bottom of the shot you can see how the headlights were attached so they could swivel – see opposite for how this worked. By the right one you can just make out the small oil can with its tube for routine maintenance.

FORD GP

Some people might think this a daft idea, but in fact it was a surprisingly effective and sensible alternative. To drive now, it feels a little odd but at reasonable speeds it settles down almost exactly like a normal vehicle. It certainly doesn't sway around. Yet at low speeds it feels like its simply turning on its own length. If you were stuck in a narrow lane with an enemy tank ahead traversing its gun towards you, and you needed to get turned round fast and away, you'd want one of these.

This was a neat and simple idea. The headlight was bolted to an arm which was hinged at the front and held by a wingnut at the back. Used like this it was a normal headlight. But if you simply spun off the wingnut you could turn the headlight round so that it could be used to illuminate the engine bay when working on it. The cable was made long enough to reach at full swivel.

WARTIME JEEPS

Looking very similar to the earlier Budd version, the GP's dashboard and driving position hasn't improved much. The handbrake is still on the floor, cluttering up the space on top of that bulbous transmission tunnel, along with the main gearlever, and levers for transfer case and front axle lock. Fabulous steering wheel – far too expensive to last.
This model features a period fire extinguisher strapped to the transmission tunnel. The brass finish to the fire extinguisher would clearly stand out on a sunny day, but it was not until about June 1942 that the various suppliers of the extinguishers like The General Fire Truck Corporation or, unusually, the English Pyrene company, started to supply them painted olive drab.

Dials almost identical to the Budd. Note how on the speedometer the different operational speeds are marked for each gear. With no rev counter, and big boots on the throttle, it was at least something to try and stick to. The T-button on the right is the hand throttle, and the C-button on the left is the choke. Below that is the lights switch obscured by the gearlever.

42

FORD GP

Close-up showing the headlights protected within the grille, with the blackout lights just in front. On the other side was the horn, also behind the grille. Note the rare green rubber bonnet blocks. Once Japan started conquering much of South East Asia, rubber became too valuable to use for things like this and they were replaced with wood and canvas, starting in September 1942, nearly a year after this Jeep was produced. Despite the lighter load and weight of the mudguards, a bracing strut remains.

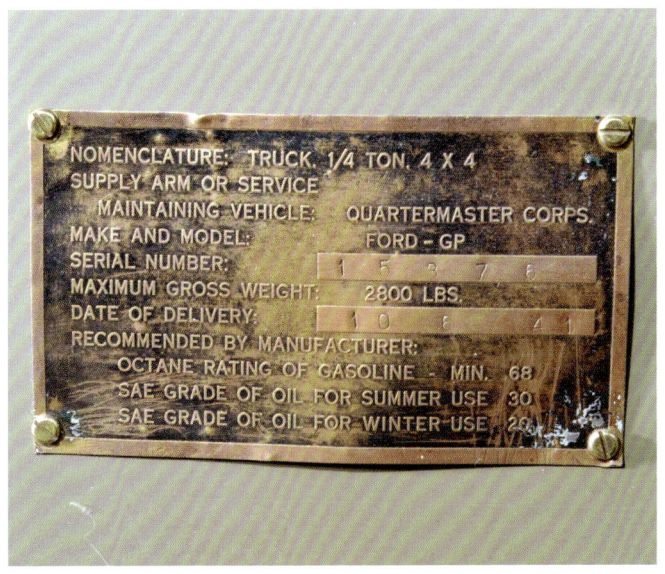

Delivered in October 1941, another ¼-ton truck for the Quartermaster Corps. All the Ford GP bodies were made by Budd, who built the prototype featured in Chapter 1.

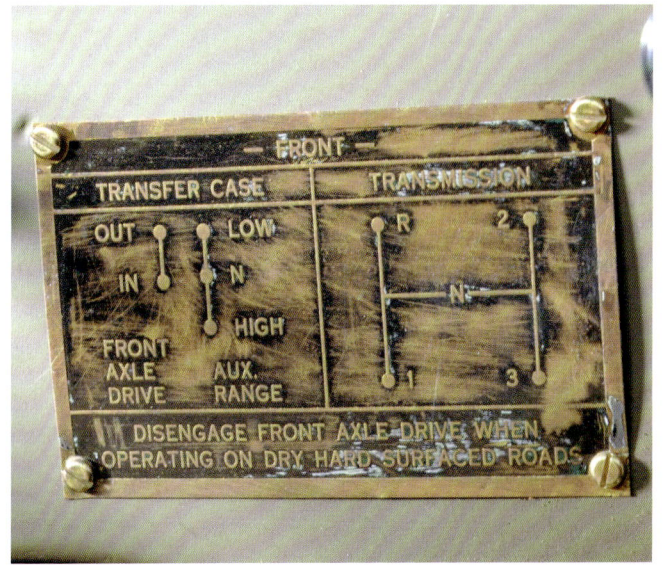

WARTIME JEEPS

The florid Ford script, or at least the "F", was found stamped all over the Ford-produced vehicles until eventually the Army became tired of rival manufacturers using their vehicles for free advertising and stopped the practice. Note the rubber seal around the tail lights. Again, due to shortages, this was phased out by Willys around September 1942 and slightly later by Ford when their stocks were exhausted.

The passenger seat could simply swivel forward. Underneath was strapped the entire canvas top, readily accessible if it came on to rain suddenly. At least, that was the theory.

Lift out the seat squab and under the driver's seat was the fuel tank, with the filler easily accessible. However, it was probably not the most relaxing thing to sit on when going in to combat.

This shot shows how the floorpan had to be adapted to take the four-wheel steering. Just behind the passenger seat you can see where the straight lines have had to be compromised so that the rear wheels underneath could clear the bodywork at full extension.
If you compare this shot to the same one of the Budd you'll notice how much smaller the grab handles are on this. The stowage bins at the rear are still a good size and feature metal instead of wooden lids. The seats still offer quite a lot of lateral support, which is nice when you're in them, not so nice when you need to get out in a hurry. Padding over the metal sides would have helped, as here, but eventually the whole lot disappeared. Note the simpler assembly appearing to hold the rear bench seat. The base can still fold up, but does so with a simpler tubular frame.

Chapter 5
WILLYS MB

By the end of World War II Willys had produced 361,339 Jeeps. Over a third of a million vehicles, more even than the mighty Ford industrial complex could match. And this is what they made in overwhelming numbers, the Willys MB. If you flick back to the Willys MA you can fairly easily spot the major differences and similarities but it must be remembered that this was a vehicle produced during a war. One result is that the vehicle was constantly evolved, with tiny and even larger items being updated and altered as the long production run went on. They didn't herald a new model, like they would with a modern car, every time they changed a body panel or added a waterproofed speedo.

One major change that is easily spotted is that, for a while, Willys continued with the welded front grille that they had used on the MA. From the outset the MB used the flat bonnet which Ford had designed, with the headlamps now incorporated into the grille. The grille, made up of arc-welded iron bars, was heavy and prone to breakage so during March 1942 Willys switched from this design to a grille made of a stamped steel section.

These early models featuring the iron bars are known as "slat grille" MBs. The first 25,808 Willys MB models were of this slat grille design – that number is included in the total above. The first 20,698 MBs didn't have a glovebox fitted either, so very few slat grille MBs have a stowage area in front of the passenger.

Inside the Jeep, further improvements can be seen compared to the MA. The gearlever moved from the steering column to the floor, next to the other levers for two-speed transfer case and front axle lock. This made driving a Jeep less "different" for military drivers who had to get used to hopping in to a range of vehicles.

The handbrake also moved from the driver's left side to the dash between the seats, following the thinking that, in an emergency, it gave the passenger some chance of yanking on the handbrake if the driver was drunk, shot or suffering any of the thousand outcomes for a combat soldier.

The driver's seat was right above the fuel tank. On the MA this had a capacity of 10 gallons but the designers sensibly increased this to 15 gallons (US gallons) and added as standard the five-gallon fuel can on the rear panel. In effect this doubled the range offered by the MB over the MA, again a potentially vital statistic given that jungles and deserts don't always have conveniently placed fuel stations.

It's noticeable how virtually all the changes to production are improvements that reflected life in the real world of combat. For example, during 1942 Willys switched wheels to a split-rim wheel with 6.00 x 16 tyres, which allowed the wheel to run flat for a while. Virtually all but the first MBs were fitted with these, allowing the Jeeps to keep moving even when under fire and with the tyres hit.

Further practical thinking replaced the ignition key with a handle-type ignition switch. This meant that soldiers could no longer wander off with the keys, immobilising the Jeep. By December 1942 Willys had moved production over to keyless ignition.

The stripped-down philosophy had been built into the Jeep. In reality, its occupants had little more weather protection than a motorcyclist, except they didn't get the special clothing. The two tubular-framed front seats and the bench rear seat were covered in heavyweight, water-repellent cotton duck material. Beneath that material, the seating itself got less and less luxurious as the war wore on and shortages became a problem. Originally filled with 2in foam rubber, the seats' interiors was replaced with a cattle-hair pad covered in rubber before even that rubber element disappeared to be replaced by some springing. The cold, uncomfortable seating, often wet, combined with the harsh ride, particularly in the rear, led to a lot of ailments for crews exposed to these conditions for long. Things like piles were known as "the Jeep disease".

Over the whole interior could go a canvas hood assembly. On the MA this was supported by a single cross brace of tubular section metal. On the MB this was increased to two braces, which managed to make the structure a bit more robust and also increased headroom without increasing the height of the silhouette.

On the rear went a government-standard plug connector socket for the taillights on the standard quarter-ton trailer. While this and the other modifications mentioned were all practical and sensible, the one side-effect was that they ramped up the Willys MB's weight. Ironic, given the efforts that had been made to shed that weight to win the contract. In fact the final weight of an MB was 2554lbs.

The original weight limit, as laid in the original specifications, had been just 1300lbs, but nobody could get near that and it had been raised to 2150lbs for the final specification. So the actual mass-produced Jeep was still some 400lbs over the limit. But it didn't matter. The Jeep could still do more than anyone had ever envisaged, and would be one of the most important workhorses of the war.

The workers on the numerous assembly lines were fired by the knowledge that their creation was helping to win the war and make solders' lives just that little bit better all over the planet. The company could bask in the patriotic knowledge that they were doing their part. And Willys could further bask in the knowledge that the contract with the government paid them $739 per vehicle.

The MB hood had two internal hoops compared to the one on the MA. This allowed a bit more headroom without raising the silhouette. As you can see, the various panels were strapped onto small handles around the outside of the vehicle, and went over clips on the front screen frame. Although it looks cosy, in cold weather this didn't keep the cold out, and the constant flapping when moving could become irritating. This shot shows the torque-reaction leaves under the engine on the driver's side. The Willys ran Kelsey-Hayes split-rim combat wheels. These replaced the one-piece wheels which were used prior to February 1942.

WARTIME JEEPS

Side view shows the effect of the two hoops that helped support the canvas top. With this layout the main top panel has been joined by the two main rear panels, which are tied into place. There are two further panels, with clear plastic and canvas, one for each door, which are not in place. Compared to, say, the shots of the Ford GPW with everything folded flat on pages 67-68, it's clear that this is a significantly higher silhouette. There were times when keeping the rain off came second to avoiding the eyes of the artillery spotters. On the near wing you can see the large blackout light with its attendant metal hoop.

Good view of the stamped metal grille which replaced the slat grille on the MBs. The first 25,808 MBs had the slat grille before production switched to this stamped steel one-piece unit. All MBs had the flat Ford-inspired bonnet rather than the raised unit seen on the MA. The capstan winch was an original option although the dent in the bumper is a more recent addition. The radiator condenser tank above the winch was originally a modification carried out in the desert, but it proved popular in other theatres. Note the wooden bonnet blocks replacing the more valuable rubber units found on earlier Jeeps.

WILLYS MB

The capstan winch could be used for a variety of purposes, from clearing trees across the road to winching the Jeep up a steep slope. It ran off the engine and so it was important that the engine speed didn't rise too far. As the plate says, it had to be kept below 1200rpm and was controlled by the hand throttle on the dashboard. The green metal strip between the winch and the sign is to stop the winch accidentally being engaged by the black knob at the top. Just behind the grille is the tubular front crossmember, to which the grille is bolted.

Good shot of the blackout light and its protecting hoop. At least there was plenty of room up there where the original headlights had been on earlier models. Sadly the bumper damage is relatively recent, a memento of a 3000-mile trip round Alaska – the Jeep in front failed on a hill climb and came down backwards rather faster than anyone was anticipating! Given that a Jeep hit the front with some momentum, to simply have a dent in the bumper is testament to the rugged build quality.

WARTIME JEEPS

The five-gallon fuel can became a standard fitment from March 1943, strapped to a base plate which was spot-welded to the back panel. With the larger fuel tank inside this gave a welcome increase in operating range. With spare wheel, a huge inventory of standard tools, a spade and axe and much more, a Jeep was a remarkably self-sufficient machine.

A standard-fitment axe and spade increased the chances of the crew keeping going, even in thick mud or sand. The Number 2 spade and 2.5kg axe were invariably painted the same colour as the vehicle. The fuel tank stone guard under the driver's seat can be seen here. The Willys MB's tank held 15 gallons as against the MA's 10 gallons

One of the issues with Jeeps was that the engine was set slightly off-centre on the driver's side. One of the effects was bump-steer and problems when braking hard in a straight line. The solution was to add a second spring under the driver's side of the Jeep. Comprising two leaves, it is set below and in front of the nine-leaf standard spring.

WARTIME JEEPS

There's little point in talking about the minutiae of the dials until we've dealt with the elephant in the room, in this case the Garand carbine in its holder. These gun holders started appearing on MBs in September 1943 and were attached to the windscreen panel by two brackets.

The green three-spoke steering wheel was introduced in September 1942 and had a composite rim (possibly made from soya bean extract) and metal spokes, replacing the rubber rim.

Leather gaiters on the gearlever and other levers replaced the previous rubber boots towards the end of 1942. There are some modern items here as befits a vehicle which is still road-legal and regularly used: the indicator assembly on the steering column, the fire extinguisher far right and the locked box in the middle.

Early MBs didn't have a glovebox, but this 1943 version does. To the left of it is the umbrella handle of the handbrake, with everything else in clear view of the driver.

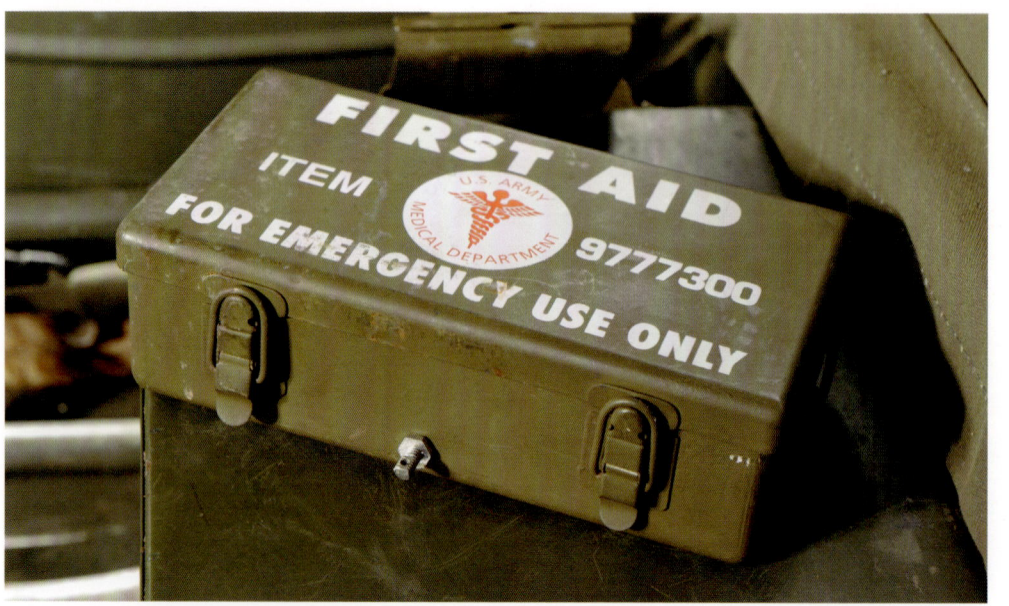

Original First Aid Kit carried all the basics you'd need in the field, but you'd hope a medic wasn't far away if the shells started falling. This tin was held on a bracket behind the dashboard, and was accessed by reaching under the dash on the passenger side.

The Go-Devil engine, still going strong in the 21st century. The oil-bath air cleaner is the black cylinder back left, which feeds across over the engine to the carburettor on the right, with the inlet and exhaust manifolds below. This standard bonnet lid shows that even the space beneath it was used. The grease gun on the right – a standard fitment from the very end of 1943 – helped with routine maintenance, and in that metal sleeve is dropped a lubrication chart, itself a metal sheet.

WARTIME JEEPS

Atmospheric shot of the interior, complete with mostly original equipment. The ammunition box between the front seats is a modern addition. The electric windscreen wipers are from a post-war French Hotchkiss Jeep and are six-volt. Rather better than trying to clear the screen by hand.

This vehicle successfully covered over 3000 miles relatively recently, when it was driven up the Alaska Highway, to the Arctic Circle and down to Anchorage. With temperatures sometimes reaching 100 degrees, the radiator condenser tank did sterling work, as did the rest of this indestructible vehicle.

The standard plates, although the shiny metal surround of the middle plate is modern, used to overcome the effects of half a century of rust. Notice how with each new model the amount of information on these plates gradually increases.

The space under the rear bench seat was fully utilised. There are clearly a couple of more recent items in there, but the big pump and valves are original. The clips to attach the pump to the underside of the seat were first introduced in December 1942.

The standard five dials. Simple, easy to read, giving enough information for the driver to keep an eye on things without being distracted. The central speedo features a black counterbalance to the white needle to give a steadier reading. This waterproof version, mostly made by King Seely, was introduced in June 1943.

… WARTIME JEEPS

Chapter 6
WILLYS MB
Long Range Desert Group

Although Jeeps were involved in every theatre of operations, their versatility and ability to cover huge distances over rough ground especially invaluable in the desert. In the awesome arena of the Sahara the Jeep wasn't the only way of getting around but it had advantages over both the German Kubelwagen and indeed the resident camels.

For those who have never been lucky enough to be in deep desert some of the stories sound rather far-fetched. How could you not see the enemy only 100 yards away in apparently featureless open ground? Could you really just appear out of the desert, shoot up a convoy and then disappear again to the extent that aircraft couldn't find you?

The desert is an extraordinary environment that seems to bend distances, colours, the horizon and even time. To survive in it you need to be many things, but the first thing you need to be is completely self-contained, especially in time of war when the few wells and oases are either under enemy control or else closely watched. Into this environment went a group of men from the Scots and Coldstream Guards, to fight the Germans and to gather information and carry out deep reconnaissance work. They were part of the Long Range Desert Group.

The LRDG was set up as an independent unit with its own spotter planes, repair vehicles and signals troops. There were two main squadrons, A and B, and within each squadron were two patrols which were themselves then sub-divided into half-patrols. What you see you here is one of the two Jeeps from B Squadron's G Patrol. This is G1, and the other half of the patrol was G2.

Each half-patrol would have had – in theory – two Jeeps, and about four Chevrolet 30cwt trucks for wireless, medical supplies, spares and heavy weapons. This meant that the Jeeps could go out from the mother ships, as it were, to patrol and do reconnaissance, and could get back without having to take too much fuel or supplies with them.

A typical mission for G1 was Operation Caravan in September 1942. About five Jeeps and 12 support trucks headed out from the LRDG headquarters south of Cairo to attack the airport and train station at Barce, which was the Italian headquarters. This was a formidable mission, and it took 12 days of hard travelling just to get there. Unfortunately the lead Jeep crashed on the way on a "blade dune" – one where you drive over only to find there's virtually nothing the other side. Both the crew were injured and could take no further part but the commander, Captain Alastair Timpson, did recover. He received a new crewman, Norman "Jack" Wheatley, and this is their vehicle, which fought through from Alamein to the end of the desert war.

This is a replica, but it's an exact replica, based on a 1942 Willys MB. How accurate is it? And is that rather odd looking paintjob remotely realistic? Put it this way, when Jack Wheatley saw it he said "You couldn't get any closer to the real thing". We even know that the paintjob was applied in Cairo in 1942 by a man with the rather wonderful name of Mohammed John.

The paintwork does look unusual and was applied with a large airbrush with the nozzle moving towards and away from the bodywork so that the strange blurry pattern emerges. Even in these photos you can see how effective it is, and that's in the very different light of England. Add in some heat haze and the vehicle disappears. The pink colour was also picked up by the SAS, since they all noticed how the light turns pink quite often towards the end of a hot day in the desert.

Unlike some of the SAS vehicles which were also in the desert, one of the most obvious points is that the Willys isn't covered in spare cans of fuel and water. Because of the way they set up operations, using the trucks not only to add firepower to any attacks but also to stand off remotely when the Jeeps were out scouting and generally being annoying to the Italians and Germans, there was no need to carry weeks of essential liquids. Instead there is an oil can beside the driver and a water can beside the passenger.

Some other remedies were cooked up in the field. One of these vehicles suffered a smashed transfer case after hitting a rock in the sand. All the oil was gone and they had none left. So they repaired the transfer case and put in banana skins – from a handy nearby banana palm oasis – and the natural oils in the skins kept them going back to base. Don't try this in your Range Rover Sport.

At the front is a modification that the SAS and others took right through to Europe in 1944 and '45 – see Chapter 11 for more. The desert gets tremendously hot – this is hardly breaking news – and an internal combustion engine produces plenty more heat. It was found that running tubing to a small external condenser tank mounted on the front helped keep the temperature down. This was linked to cutting out most of the slats on the front grille to improve airflow to the radiator.

Of course there wasn't much point in trekking for days across the desert to shoot up a vital supply route or convoy if you only had a can of bully beef to throw at the enemy when you got there. To beef up the hand-held weapons that are littered all over the vehicle, the passenger/navigator also had a pair of Vickers K guns. These carried 100-round drums and had a massive rate of fire, faster even than the German MG34.

The idea was to arrive fast, hit hard and get out fast, and the Vickers Ks certainly helped with that. Plus, if it all started to go wrong, their field of suppressive fire would keep the enemy's heads down while you had a ponder on what to do next.

With food, water, supplies, weapons, two compasses and more, the G1 Jeep was a self-contained war machine that could cross just about everything the Sahara had to throw at it, and could deliver men and material hundreds of miles from where the enemy expected. Camouflaged under scrim netting it could lie hidden close to the enemy and, for attack or retreat, it was relied on by an extraordinary band of men with their very lives.

Even in clear English light, this vehicle begins to merge into the background at a distance of only about 30m. Throw over a scrim net, take off the coloured pennant, and you'd never see it from the ground, let alone from the air.

WARTIME JEEPS

Notice how high the twin Vickers K guns are mounted. There would have been times when this would have seemed rather exposed but, if you need to elevate the barrels to engage an aircraft, then you need the room. In the desert enemy aircraft were a real and constant threat.

The Vickers K guns were originally designed for use on aircraft and were seen in everything from the Fairey Swordfish to the Bristol Blenheim bomber. When they moved to belt-fed guns these drum-magazine models were cleared for supply to special forces. The Vickers K guns had the advantage of a high rate of fire, which was ideal for hit-and-run operations, and their light, low-friction moving parts made them particularly suitable for the desert, where they didn't tend to jam as often as some other machine guns.

The data plates show this Willys MB was produced in July 1942. There were various models of glovebox lid and fastener, including a locking type, but this is the common push-button version.

It looks a bit of a shambles but actually all the things that would be needed in a hurry are close to hand. Around the front seats are spare ammunition and billy cans, water, an entrenching tool, first-aid kit and a Thompson sub-machine gun since you can never have too many. The five-gallon jerrycan is a German original, clearly marked for water so nobody puts the contents in the fuel tank. Note the sun compass placed on the dashboard to the right of the driver's position, a highly useful piece of kit for when the main magnetic compass had problems.

This is what happens when you leave chaps to do the packing. Clothing, food, drink and supplies all jumbled together. Add in constant thumps and bumps of desert travel, plus clouds of sand and dust, and the chances of laying your hands on your clean underwear were pretty remote.
Just a cursory glance through this authentic pile revealed: sleeping bags, tin hats, Schmeisser sub-machine gun (presumably taken on a raid), German beer (ditto), billycans, water bottles, a jar of rum, overcoats, scrim nets and a spade.

WARTIME JEEPS

Unlike the SAS Jeep later in Europe – see Chapter 11 – the LRDG Jeeps weren't stripped back to quite such a degree. The handles on the corners are still in place, since getting bogged down was quite likely to happen as they crossed everything from the infamous talcum-powder sand called feche-feche to actual quicksand.

Note the front tyres, which were changed to road tyres since these were found to be more effective at rolling over the sand crust instead of breaking through it. The rears were standard all-terrain tyres, as was the spare. The spare is mounted on a quickly detachable holder with just two large wingnuts to spin off so changing a wheel could be done in a hurry.

LRDG WILLYS MB

Both the LRDG and the SAS went down the route of removing most of the bars of the front grille to aid cooling, and then fitting a condenser tank to the outside – you can see the tubing running back into the radiator. By the driver is one of two compasses for instant reference, and a small can of oil with the patrol name, G1, stencilled onto it.

The P4 compass was vital when travelling for days across relatively featureless terrain, trying to keep out of the way of enemy forces until you were ready. Like so many bits of special forces kit, this compass originated with the RAF. They were found in a variety of aircraft, including the Sunderland flying boat and early bombers but, like the Vickers K guns, as they were superseded newer equipment, these older but still very serviceable compasses made their way over to the special forces.

WARTIME JEEPS

Fine shot at speed. The ride was fairly harsh even on tarmac, and over stony ground it wasn't comfortable at all, although the ride in the front was better than in the rear. The suspension took an awful beating in the desert but there were no design weaknesses, even in these extreme conditions.

Taking a break. All the uniforms and accessories are genuine, like the Jeep. The axe and spade have been relegated to the rear to make way for the vital compass and also the can of oil. A good shot of the metal protection around the fuel tank under the seat, protruding under the bodywork. The extra lengths on the barrels of the machine guns beyond the final sights/crossbrace are the muzzle blast supressors.

LRDG WILLYS MB

Your transport, your home. The Jeep was never designed to be a comfortable vehicle, so spending days on those seats would have been tough. At least the LRDG, because of their use of 30cwt trucks working in tandem with the Jeeps, meant that the Jeeps themselves didn't need to carry anything but the bare essentials. This vehicle looks heavily laden but the crew got off lightly compared to their SAS counterparts, who had to carry tens of gallons of extra fuel and gallons of extra water as well as all the kit you see here.

Good shot of the airbrush effect of the paint. Each colour could be found in the desert, depending not only on the terrain but also the time of day. The pink and the yellow, for example, could each blend into exactly the same stretch of sand, depending on whether it was early morning or late afternoon. Removing the grille bars does seem to have been effective but it also came to be a special forces trademark. Just behind the bottom of the grille can be made out the front crossmember, showing this is a Willys MB model.

63

WARTIME JEEPS

Rear view shows the twin wingnuts on the spare wheel for quick release. Note that things like the bumperettes and handles are still left in place, unlike the more stripped down SAS Jeep seen later in this book.

In September 1942, a few months after this Jeep rolled off the line, the black steering wheel was replaced with a composite green one that saved on valuable resources. The windscreen has been removed along with the wing mirror. A windscreen is a major source of glare in the desert and so would easily reflect light and tell the enemy where you were – and with a big pair of machine guns needing a clear field of fire it would have had to be folded flat the whole time anyway. There were standard issue windscreen covers to deal with the issue of glare – you can see one in place on the Ford GPW in the next chapter.

Another shot showing the difference between the front and rear tyres. The desert makes particular demands on vehicles, and keeping on the sand as opposed to sinking into it was something that crews spent a lot of time working on. Despite being laden with kit and twin machine guns, and being driven hard over thousands of miles of brutal terrain – the Sahara is as much stone as sand – these Jeeps proved reliable workhorses. They needed no special adaptations, bar the cautionary one of adding to the already impressive engine cooling system. They worked, straight out of the crate, and this one is still working many decades later.

Chapter 7
FORD GPW

Ford's involvement with the Jeep project was very stop-start right from the off. They failed to enter an initial prototype when Bantam managed it. They did produce a prototype for the final tests, having been spoon-fed a set of blueprints, but the resulting Pygmy actually came third behind Willys and Bantam. They had labour problems and supplier problems and were focused on other areas of business.

But this was Ford. When they sensed the size of the possible order base, and when they were treated as favoured supplier even by the American Quartermaster Corps, the giant began to focus. By the time of the Service Test finals they were pushing very hard to get the whole order. As mentioned earlier, for a while it looked like they were going to get it, with a vehicle that they'd copied from Bantam and then fitted with an inappropriate tractor engine.

Fortunately common sense prevailed and Willys won the first order for 16,000 units. However, disquiet had arisen right back when Bantam were the only player, a disquiet centred on the ability of anyone to produce the kind of volumes envisaged in time of war. Bantam couldn't do it, and it was felt that even Willys would struggle. So the highly unusual agreement was reached that Ford would make Jeeps too, so that effectively Ford were making Willys Jeeps.

The agreement, signed on 10 November 1941, was for an initial production of 15,000 Jeeps and Willys handed over the drawings to allow this to happen – an agreement that didn't benefit Willys financially or in any other way, but they did it anyway.

Ford was to produce a Willys MB replica, right down to the Go-Devil engine. As a sign of how odd this arrangement was, in January 1942 Ford was turning out Jeeps that had engines that had actually been made by Willys and then sent to rivals Ford while they cranked up their own production.

As we saw with the previous Ford GP model, G stood for Government contract, P was their code for one of their 80in vehicles. And now they added the W to denote Willys. Production got underway of the Ford GPW. By the time production ended, Ford had made a grand total of 277,896 GPWs to go with the 361,339 Willys MBs.

How do you tell them apart? The most obvious clue is in the front chassis crossmember, just visible in many photographs below the front grille. On the Willys this was of a curved oval shape, and on the Ford it was an inverted U shape. That grille was always made of stamped steel on the GPW, unlike the early slat-grille MBs.

One other way to tell them apart is to look in detail since, as mentioned earlier, Ford had a virtual obsession with marking items as made by Ford. Willys too liked to put its logo on things like the rear panel, although both Ford and Willys were eventually told to desist by military accountants who didn't see why the companies should have free advertising. On the Ford virtually everything had either the Ford logo or the florid F trademark. Body panels, even seals and locking washers were stamped with the corporate logo in the rather obsessive way of a cat marking its territory.

So was the Ford GPW really identical to the Willys MB? The reality is that both companies operated to the same blueprints, but both used a multitude of suppliers scattered all over America, suppliers that had to battle with wartime restrictions on raw materials and the heavy and constant demands of full-speed production year after year. There were bound to be discrepancies but in 1943 there was actually a study to see how the two compared.

A GPW and an MB were taken apart item by item and weighed, examined and judged. Unsurprisingly there weren't any major differences but there were some smaller ones, like the

FORD GPW

fact that the Ford bonnet was not as robust as the Willys one.

One more important difference hinged on the engine, the Go-Devil that Willys were so proud of. Their engine weighed 557lbs complete with transfer case, carburettor, electrics and starter. The Ford engine weighed ten pounds less in the same state, which was a worry as that didn't bode well for a robust, long-life engine. This concern was further highlighted by the fact that the Ford dipstick was set too low, thereby giving the false impression there was more oil in the engine than there actually was. Although this was rectified, there does seem to be some evidence to suggest that Ford engines generally didn't last as long as the Willys-built units.

Clearly the point of the exercise was to ensure commonality of parts so that if a Jeep in theatre needed, say, a new engine, it shouldn't matter if it was a GPW or an MB or whether Ford or Willys had made the engine. One outcome of the comparison study was to find that the Warner Gear Company, which made the two-speed transfer case, was making the sliding gear on the Willys transfer case output shaft slightly too large for the Ford transfer case output shaft, and so minor adjustments were made.

Ford always tried to use as many of their own components as possible. For example their Dearborn factory churned out the 6.00x16 non-directional tyres used on every Jeep, but in December 1942 the American government bought the whole factory and shipped it out to Russia to help our new allies. This left an annoyed Ford with no tyre manufacturer of their own, so they had to go to Firestone and other manufacturers for tyres for the rest of the war.

Overall, the Willys and Ford deal was a triumph of co-operation and logistics on an unimaginable scale. One certainly couldn't imagine such a situation unless they'd been forced into it by war. Even during the war Willys-Overland was advertising in the USA, reminding people that not only was the Jeep powered by a Willys-Overland engine, but that the very name Jeep was a Willys-Overland trademark – and nothing to do with Ford.

Atmospheric shot of the GPW looking low and ready to go. The side door canvas has been joined by a canvas cover for the windscreen. This could be fairly quickly drawn over the screen, where its purpose was to ensure there was no glare from the glass, which might alert enemy troops or aircraft.

WARTIME JEEPS

With the screen down the Jeep presented a low silhouette, and of course if there were something like a big .50-cal machine gun mounted centrally, it would need the screen down for a clear field of fire. All Ford GPWs used split-rim combat wheels, as here, which meant they could run flat for a while. The 6.00-16 tyres ran non-directional tread (NDT) and were made by a variety of manufacturers.

Standard five-gallon can filling up the 15-gallon tank under the seat. To do this the driver had to take off the seat base, unscrew the filler cap, pull out the pouring tube which you see sitting proud of the seat, and then pour in the fuel via an extended nozzle which often lived just to the bottom right of this shot, behind the spade.

FORD GPW

Engine in sound working order. Ford made these engines to the Willys blueprint, but there were marginal differences. Overall, the Ford engine was ten pounds lighter than the Willys version, which raises questions about longevity – in theory at least. This particular engine has done over 100,000 miles with the same owner since he bought it in 1969 and has only been rebuilt once.

The Ford bonnet tended not to be quite as robust as the Willys bonnet. Again, you can see the grease-gun in place as well as the lubrication chart sticking out of its metal holder. Dog is contemporary.

WARTIME JEEPS

Stripped back to the minimum of canvas. If you look at the front cross-member, just visible below the front grille, you can see it is of an inverted-U shape and flat across, unlike the curved tubular section used in the Willys. Note the large blackout light on the front mudguard, with its own guard.

Spring–loaded cover top left is for the standard electrical socket that could connect to the quarter-ton trailer. Below that, the yellow glass in the light is post-war. Good detail of the QMC – Quartermaster Corps stamped on the fuel can. By this stage the bumperettes were a standard size, as here.

70

FORD GPW

Original felt between the radiator front and the grille.

Oil can and spout live just to the left of the horn inside the engine bay, conveniently placed for use.

A view of the front nearside suspension, with extra leaves to help with the overall balance and handling. Ford usually used Gabriel-made shock absorbers.

71

WARTIME JEEPS

Original bonnet block for when the bonnet was raised and leant against the windscreen. Rubber had been replaced by wood and, in this case, canvas infill, since about September 1942.

A typical example of Ford marking everything it could with its own logo – in this case the blackout light. These large units started to appear on the GPWs from November 1942.

Detail of the stowage bin in the rear. The metal chute that you can see is there to protect the trailer wiring.

The original jack would also live in one of these stowage bins.

72

The standard spade and axe are joined here by the spare fuel can nozzle, which slots neatly into place. Note the original seat cushions. They had zips in so that soldiers could put extra stuffing in there for comfort, particularly their blanket, but by about July 1943 – some months after this vehicle came off the line – the practice was stopped as the soldiers simply didn't seem to be making use of this.

Looking down at the front bumper you can see the block of wood which was often placed behind the metal bumper to add strength. A rope was often looped over this, ready to be quickly used.

WARTIME JEEPS

Entrenching tool sits on the rear bench seat. Behind the back of the seat the starting handle was kept, with the toolkit under the base. These are original seats and have animal hair and metal springs inside, which offered limited comfort over any great distance.

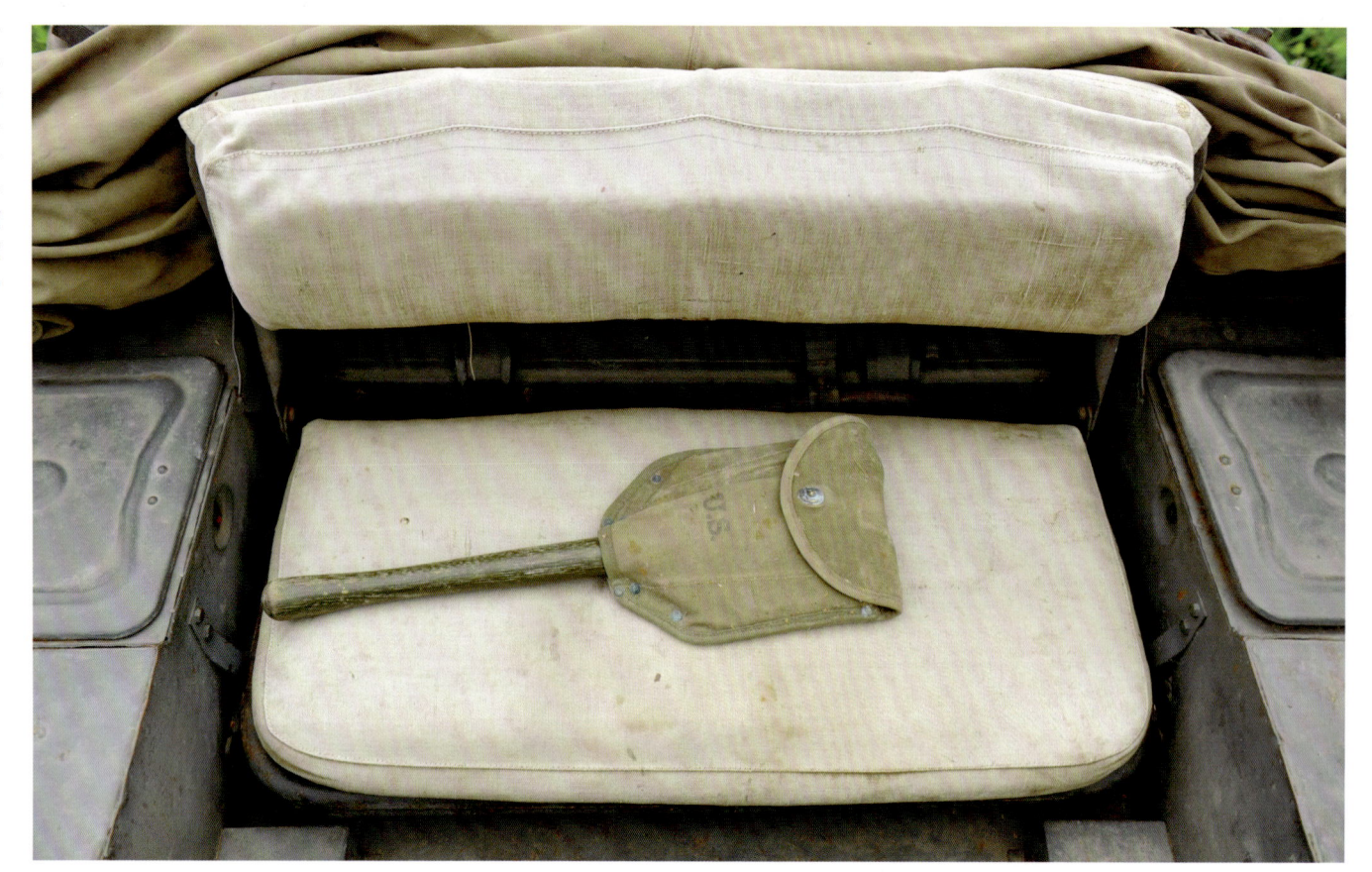

With the base of the seat lifted, you can see the big pump which was stowed out of the way. More tools could be stored in this space.

FORD GPW

This is virtually identical to the Willys MB dash, and in this case even includes the gun holder in front of the wheel. Ford used cast-iron pedals while Willys used stamped steel.

Note that this model had the plates displayed on the glovebox. The glovebox itself was held by a catch rather than a lock, and all GPWs were fitted with this glovebox which, in theory, held official items like gas masks and eye shields.

75

WARTIME JEEPS

The spare fuel can became a standard fitment. It sat in its holder and was then strapped into place with a webbing strap which was riveted to the base. Note the towhook, bottom right, which was a cast item at this stage before moving over to a pressed hook.

The flexible radio antenna was bolted to various different places on the Jeep, in this case by the rear wheel. The name Ohio Brass can just be made out on the base.

Again, virtually identical dials to the Willys. In this case the Ford speedometer is slightly different and also features a tripmeter as well as a mileometer.

FORD GPW

Side doors made at least an attempt at keeping mud and water out of the vehicle when going along. They poppered into place but obviously didn't help with getting in and out. Note the exhaust exiting on the passenger side. This was partly because of the bigger fuel tank, which was L-shaped, pushing the exhaust out the other side.

A retro-fitted windscreen wiper mechanism. This became available in 1944 and was fitted to some Jeeps. It was a vacuum wiper with a pickup coming off the exhaust manifold. The original reason for the manual wiper was that it would be easier to lay the screen flat or to stack Jeeps for transport one on top of each other, if there wasn't any complex wiring to connect screen with body.

Chapter 8
FORD GPA

When you're dwarfed by a duck things aren't going that well. But that is what happened to the General Purpose Amphibious Jeep, or GPA. While the mighty DUKW ploughed on, the GPA was left in its wake, taking on water.

This is peculiar because the hulls of both amphibious vehicles were designed by the same man, naval architect Roderick Stephens. But the DUKW went on to greatness under the ownership of General Motors, arch-rivals to Ford, who produced the far less successful GPA. Part of the problem was that the GPA was designed around the Ford GPW. In itself this wouldn't be an issue but the designs were drawn up around the blueprints of a GPW not an actual vehicle. And, as we know, the weight of an actual vehicle was considerably more than the theoretical weight.

But the theory was a sound one. A Jeep that could cross land and water would be a fabulous troop carrier and reconnaissance vehicle. The original design was worked up by Marmon-Herrington and the boat builders Sparkman and Stephens while Ford worked on their own version. In trials the Ford performed better and won the contract.

Production started in September 1942. But just nine months later, in June 1943, production stopped. By that time 12,774 vehicles had come off the production line. The lines were configured for other vehicles and no more GPAs were produced.

The problem was the weight of the vehicle, which meant that on land it seemed a bit underpowered and on water there simply wasn't enough freeboard. Although the GPA was often known as the Seep – a sea-going Jeep – the sea was not the best environment for it. Anything other than a light chop or swell would swamp the vehicle. Even so, GPAs were used successfully on D-Day, ferrying men and supplies ashore from the ships standing out to sea.

So, if not the sea, then the GPA should have come into its own during the many river crossings that the troops faced fighting through Europe. But most of the European rivers were formidable obstacles. Having run for centuries through the landscape they were sunk deep into the land, like the sunken lanes that caused the Allies such heartache in the bocage of Normandy. The rivers had steep banks in and out, often with deep mud, with the enemy well entrenched on the far bank.

Put simply, they were a killing ground, and the Allies suffered heavy casualties crossing most of them. And they did so usually without the Seeps. The steep banks were simply too much for the GPAs, which in theory could use their anchors as ground anchors, and then winch themselves up the banks. This theory worked so long as the nice men of

A Ford GPA on US Army manoeuvres with surf shield down and sidescreens in place.

FORD GPA

the 2nd SS Panzer Division opposite held their fire or considerately helped with sorting out the winch cables.

However, in the Far East and particularly in Russia, the GPAs finally proved their worth. The shallower, large rivers in Russia and Eastern Europe proved ideal for the Ford Seep, and the many that went there under the terms of Lend-Lease did sterling work throughout the war as reconnaissance vehicle and allowed bridgeheads to be formed over the rivers before the enemy had time to react.

So what was it? Basically it was a Jeep that could go on water. The dashboard looks alarmingly complex for a rookie driver, but in many ways it was a simple vehicle. For example, when driving along the road, the rudder still turned every time the steering wheel turned.

Naturally all the steel bodywork, pumps, props and all the rest add to the weight. With a road-going weight of 3400lbs, the GPA was about 1000lbs heavier than the GPW. The Go-Devil engine was a strong performer but, with no added horsepower, it struggled to deal effectively with that much weight.

The engine was in the bows, between the front wheels. The gearbox was to the rear of the engine with the transfer

Seeps being field-tested by Ford on the Rouge River adjacent to the sprawling Rouge complex in Dearborn, Michigan.

box. Off this there were two levers, which were to the driver's right, one bringing in the prop, the other the bilge pump. A lever by the passenger seat could switch the bilge pump to either the front or the rear bilges.

To bring the prop in, when the driver went from land to water, he had to depress the clutch and then knock the lever nearest to him behind the main gearlever. The prop speed was governed by the gearbox and engine speed. As mentioned, steering was constant, whether to the wheels or the rudder and, since the wheels continued to be driven in the water, they provided added impetus and a small amount of extra steering. The rudder was moved by two cables which ran back from the steering through quite complex pulleys to the rudder itself.

Before the GPA went into the water it was imperative to ensure the front end was secure. This meant swivelling down the surf shield and locking it in place. Behind it, there was a flap which could be opened or shut on the deck top. When open, with the breakwater swung back onto the deck behind it, there was a good flow of air for the radiator and the air filter suction pipe. Clearly this all had to be shut down when going into the water. Cooling air passed through the engine bay and out of the mesh outlets on the bows of the cockpit either side.

There was a long exhaust system which came out across the engine and then down to vent below water level on the passenger side. Further back on the passenger side, in front of the rear wheels, was another hole in the bodywork, which was for a manual starting handle.

The fuel tank, batteries (there would have been two six-volt batteries) and all the tools lived in the rear to help balance the craft.

Inside there was room for five soldiers including the driver. The driver had an adjustable seat, the only one in a Jeep, and all the seats had base squabs which had "life preserver" on them, although they'd have only offered minimal flotation for a soldier with kit on.

With an anchor to the rear, which was effectively as much a ground anchor as a sea anchor, and with capstan winch on the front, in theory the GPA was fairly self-contained, although as we've seen the theory wasn't the same as reality. Perhaps the greatest accolade to the GPA is that the Russians found it such a useful vehicle that, in the 1950s, they made their own version called the GAZ-46 MAV.

Most military vehicles were designed and built with the thought that they were disposable and most had a life expectancy measured in weeks. It is more remarkable then that the vehicle you see on the following pages was built during the Second World War but up until 1987 was still working – in the water. For decade after decade a small flotilla of GPAs were used by a family of fishermen in Scotland to work their nets in the freezing, salty sea and in the rivers that fed into the sea. It's fair to say they weren't pampered, but instead were worked hard and maintained only to a basic level, yet after some extensive rebuilding, this particular vehicle looks as good as new.

FORD GPA

On a still lake with no gunfire or waves, this looks good, but it's obvious that a swell hitting that front wouldn't have to be that big before it swept over the surf shield. The exhaust blowing into the water can be seen just this side of the front wheel. Maximum speed on water was 5.5mph and 50mph on land.

WARTIME JEEPS

The driver not only got an adjustable seat, he also got a vacuum-powered windscreen wiper – you can see the mechanism at the top of the screen, with the tube leading down the frame into the engine bay. The passenger had the usual Ford manual wiper. Below that is the gun holder, which on most Jeeps was inverted instead of open like this. Interior is relatively spacious for a Jeep, with 50ins of extra length and 7ins of extra width, at 64ins. The shiny pipe next to the driver's seat is the outlet from the bilge pump, which discharged water from front and rear bilges.

Note that it doesn't claim to be a life saver, but just a life preserver. The seat cushions could be quickly unclipped and used as a buoyancy aid if it all went wrong. Since the GPA was hardly designed as a deep-sea vessel, land wasn't usually far away.

82

FORD GPA

To a rookie driver this must have looked terrifying. For on-road use it was pretty straightforward, with the usual five dials in the centre., plus a volt meter to the right of them, the three main foot pedals and the gearlever next to him. The handbrake in the dashboard would also be familiar, as would the two levers to the right of the gearlever. The left one is to engage the front axle and the lever beside it is to engage the two-speed transfer case for either high or low ratios – identical to a normal Jeep. Less familiar would be the mass of instructions and the two further levers near the bottom of the photo. The left one is for engaging and disengaging the propeller, the right one is for engaging or disengaging the bilge pump. Just out of sight to the right of that lever is a further lever to activate the bilge pump for front or rear scavenging.

The dials are standard GPW but the instructions above the speedo tell the driver how to use the two levers for propeller and bilge pump – not something a driver on a GPW normally had to worry about. Below the volt meter the large black shiny knob is for the winch control on the front. Pushed in like this it kept the winch disengaged while pulling it fully out engaged the winch.

WARTIME JEEPS

The surf shield had to be flipped over the bow when the GPA went into the water. With it hinged back onto the deck and the air intakes open, the vehicle was ready for driving on the road.

The GPA was 182ins long, compared to a normal Jeep's 132ins, with a wheelbase of 84ins, 4ins longer than a GPW. The reinforced rib design of the hull can clearly be seen in this shot. The small hole in front of the rear wheel is where the starting handle went in to hand-start the engine. From March 1943 the manual starter was moved inboard when it was realised that there would be a problem if the battery died while the GPA was afloat. The exit of the exhaust pipe can also be seen in front of the front wheel. The canvas sections were there to act as spray guards and could be quickly taken down.

FORD GPA

With the rear seats raised, there was access to the fuel tank, the batteries and tools. The fuel filler tube is visible top right of the fuel tank. Despite the extra weight and higher fuel consumption, the tank held the same 15 US gallons as a normal Jeep.

With the seats in their normal position, the four fasteners that snap each seat to the bulkhead behind the seats and to the rail to the front of the seats are clearly visible. Because of the rear wheelarches intruding, the outside seats had limited legroom.

WARTIME JEEPS

The rear held the main fuel tank as well as the auxiliary can, partly to help counter-balance the engine in the bows. This shot shows the difficulties the designers had to face, with things like the spare tyre for the road but a long boat hook for use in the water. Ford used its split-rim combat wheels on all GPAs.

The Go-Devil engine, as made by Ford and as modified for the GPA. Most of the changes occurred back from the gear-box, but the main visible difference here is the pulley for the front winch drive – the wheel, belt and shaft heading towards the winch are clearly visible in this shot. At the base of the winch drive, which is the black unit behind the pulley, note the black rod running back towards the cabin above the cylinder head. This is the winch control rod, which ran through into the dashboard.

86

All set for the road. Although it looks quite large here, it must be remembered that this is based on a quarter-ton road vehicle, whereas the more successful DUKW weighed two and a half tons and dwarfed the GPA.

With the inspection panel up between the front seats, you can see the belt which takes power from the transfer case to the bilge pump. A pipe from the bilge entered the pump and then another pipe above it discharged the bilge water out of an exit by the driver's side.

WARTIME JEEPS

The only Jeep that can do this and not sink to the bottom. Good shot of the spare fuel holder plate. Note the leaf springs visible inboard of the wheels and the rudder with propeller behind it. The ribbing inside the propeller tunnel was there to strengthen the structure against the forces exerted by the propeller churning round in the tunnel. At this point the driver is still sending drive to the wheels but as soon as the vehicle is floating he will send drive to the propeller.

FORD GPA

The propeller is providing drive and directing the water over the rudder, while at the same time all four wheels continue to churn round providing additional drive and some steering. With just one person on board and no extra equipment you can see how low the vehicle sits in calm water.

Spare wheel and spare fuel at the stern – note the robust fuel can holder. Behind the can the protruding tube is the filler for the fuel tank beneath. The Danforth anchor was for mooring in water but was more usually used as a ground anchor to haul the GPA up banks or through particularly muddy sections.

WARTIME JEEPS

The propeller tunnel in close-up. Even with the strengthening ribs seen here, it was found in use that the forces generated by the propeller turning at speed were damaging the tunnel. So from January 1943 the metal used in this whole area was strengthened.

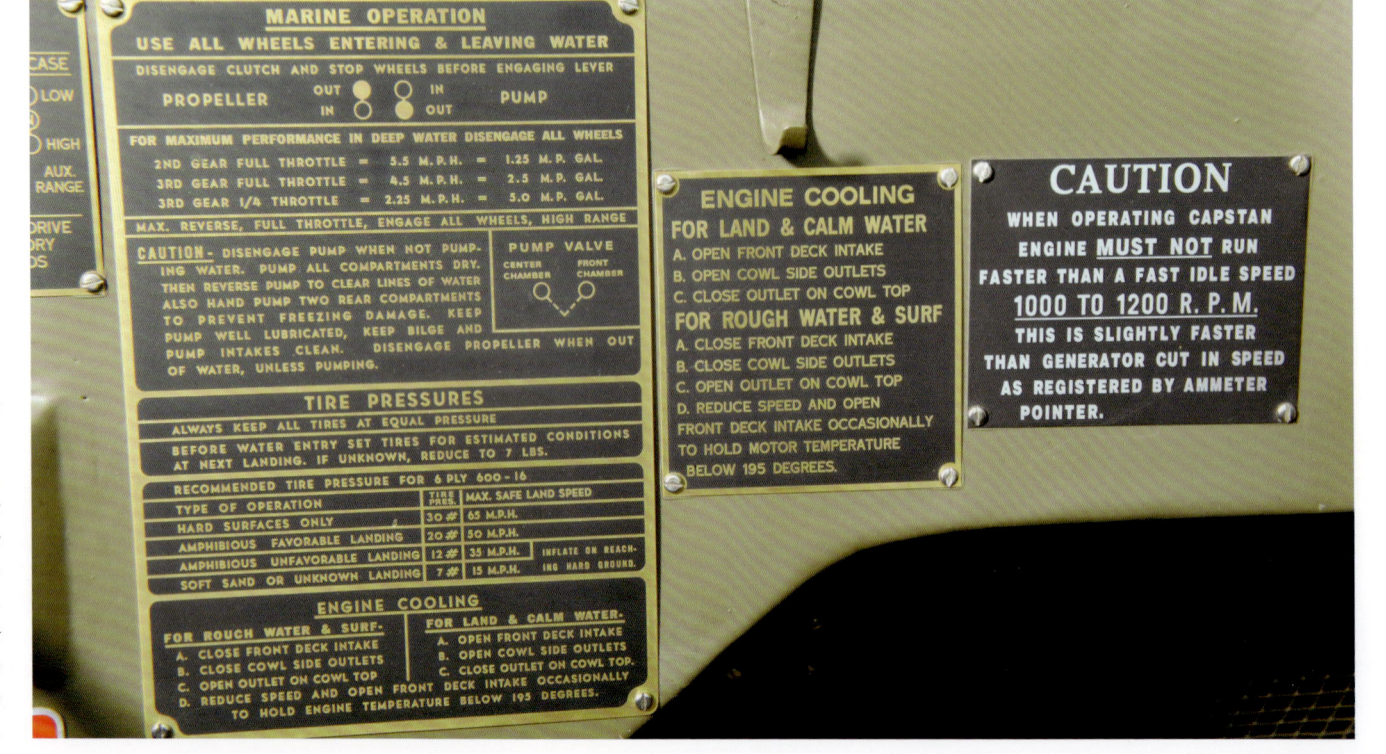

Enough to make your head spin. Pump, reverse pump, close intakes, open cowl, don't run the engine fast. But if the instructions weren't followed various calamities could befall, from overheating the engine, burning out the winch and seizing the bilge pump to actually sinking the craft.

Making a clean exit. Although it's obviously roughly made with thick steel, the hull has basically sound aquadynamic properties and would allow for getting into and out of reasonably steep rivers, just not the usually canal-like rivers found in Western Europe. This GPA would have been driving the wheels for a couple of seconds at this point, allowing a smooth exit with no need to actually stop the vehicle's progress.

Chapter 9

WILLYS MT-TUG

Four wheels good – six wheels better? That was certainly what Ford and Willys thought, almost as soon as the first prototypes were being put through their paces. By July 1941, the same month as Willys signed the first contract to produce the Willys MB, a 6x6 version of the Jeep was delivered for inspection. Even though this was fast thinking and acting by Willys, they'd been beaten to it by Ford who produced a version several months earlier. Another race looked like being on.

But it was Willys that made the running. The basic idea was to make a gun carrier that could take a 37mm cannon. While a standard MB could be adapted for all sorts of purposes, carrying something as large as a 37mm gun, associated ammunition and strengthening to cope with the recoil was too much to ask. So a 6x6 version of the Willys was created and then tested. This first model, the T-14, was then followed by the T-14a, but neither found particular favour and both were outclassed by the eventually much more successful Dodge Weapons Carrier.

But Willys kept on trying to make a successful combination of assets and next tried an armoured version, the T-24. Unsurprisingly, since this still had the almost standard Go-Devil engine, it didn't work well as it was underpowered for the extra weight. This then became a field ambulance, and then the MT-CA3 which was a cargo and troop carrier. None of these took off but, eventually, Willys progressed to the MT-TUG in early 1943.

This was more like it. It was developed for the US Army Air Corps and then the US Marines and, although it weighed three quarters of a ton, the needs of these mobile corps were clearly in the designers' minds. The Marine Corps needed mobility, both in the sense of being able to get around various battlegrounds in different theatres, but also in the sense of being able to rapidly move men and materiel from one location to another in a hurry.

At first glance this 6x6 looks like a long, quite tall vehicle but it could easily fit into a glider or be stacked one on top of another for transport from one battle zone to another. Naturally the windscreen would fold flat, and then the wooden sides at the rear could be simply lifted out of the metal slots they stood in. That left the tallest part of the vehicle as the steering wheel, and that too could be telescoped down on its column while the steering wheel itself could be angled from 45 degrees to horizontal. With large carrying rings already installed front and rear, ready to be lifted by a crane, the MT-TUG was good to go.

However there was no mistaking that this was a lot bigger than a normal Jeep – it had to be to fulfil its role. The wheelbase was 110ins, 30ins longer than standard. Width at 63ins was 6ins wider than a Willys MB. And the length of 170.5ins made it 38ins longer overall. A trailer socket was fitted as standard along with the brakes for a trailer as it was envisaged the 6x6 would be able to haul a lot of kit.

Yet the engine pulling all this was the standard Go-Devil 2.2-litre four-pot, albeit with slightly lower gearing. It had extra weight and size to haul around as well as having to deal with increased energy losses caused by the complex drivetrain.

For this was a true six-wheel drive vehicle. The rear four drove permanently and there was an axle lock to bring in the front steering pair. The rear axles had their suspension coupled together with extra support between the axles. It was a complicated and power-draining set-up but it did allow the vehicle to plough on through some pretty heavy going. Each rear axle had its own propshaft, with the rearmost axle offset to the driver's side so that the two propshafts could come down the middle of the vehicle between the frame rails.

The resulting vehicle is quite easy to drive over tough terrain – even now, many decades later, it provides a gentle, go-anywhere performance and the extra size isn't particularly apparent. The driver sat surprisingly low in the vehicle, as did the front passenger.

This was partly because the fuel tank was no longer under the driver's seat. Instead it was placed between the two front seats. Although it's the standard 15-gallon size, it looks absolutely enormous when fully visible and takes up a lot of room in the cockpit. Presumably, because of the extensive drive system, there simply wasn't room for it underneath. Instead the steering box is visible under the driver's side front wing. Or it may have been because of a desire to lower the silhouette.

Just to the rear of the fuel tank was a red lever in a circular housing. This was the lever for the electric control of the trailer brakes. Again, a complex system, but necessary to get this three-quarter ton vehicle stopped safely with half a dozen men on board and a trailer full of kit.

In the rear were bench seats down each side. In this particular manifestation, there was no central pintle for a large gun, so instead it was designed for transporting men and kit. It doesn't actually look terribly comfortable, and the driving position is certainly not one you'd want to adopt for that many hours, but this wasn't designed for trundling across Europe, it was designed to be flown in to a forward base and then used to deploy men and materiel into combat.

Despite all the undoubted good design and clear thinking that went into the Willys 6x6, it still struggled to find favour. Altogether about 15 vehicles were produced, so things clearly got beyond the basic prototype stage. It was the only 6x6 Jeep to actually carry factory serial numbers so production was clearly envisaged.

However an order for mass production eluded this interesting vehicle, and the minimal production stopped in April 1943. It could have formed the basis of a whole family of vehicles, including troop carriers, ambulances, anti-tank units and so on, but the Dodge Weapons Carrier was already well established. Lack of any kind of weather protection and, indeed, any spare wheel can't have helped but Willys believed in the vehicle enough to try and gain a patent on it in 1942, a patent which eventually failed along with the vehicle.

The very early versions of the 6x6 had the slat grille, but this later model has the more usual mass-production stamped steel grille. Good view of the front axle and steering arms. Note how the bonnet does not flow neatly into the widened body at the bulkhead. The turning circle was a fairly large 45ft.

WARTIME JEEPS

The driver and passenger sat very low, keeping the silhouette down. This was made possible by moving the 15-gallon fuel tank to sit between the front seats. This gave a range of about 300 miles. The filler cover is visible on the top of the tank. When the bullets started to fly this might not have seemed a wonderful arrangement. Just behind the fuel tank is the red lever of the electric braking system for when a trailer was behind - complex but necessary. Braking was by 9in drums with an 8in drum transmission brake on the transfer case. The round button on the floor to the front of the trailer brake is actually the horn, which had to be moved from the centre of the steering wheel for obvious reasons.

If you look at the previous photo you can see the lever on the steering column in a downward position. When it was moved horizontally towards the dials, the whole steering column could be telescoped downwards. Again, compared to the previous photo, you can see that if you pull out the two circular pins either side of the steering wheel boss, it is possible to tilt the steering wheel down to horizontal. With the back slats out and the windscreen flat, you now have a very low vehicle for transporting or stacking.

WILLYS MT-TUG

The suspension at the front included the normal telescopic dampers, visible inside the front wheel. The normal Jeep front end fits slightly uncomfortably with the wider chassis but includes all the usual attributes, like the blackout light on the near wing. Also visible is one of the two rings on the front end for quick lifting.

WARTIME JEEPS

Axle articulation can be usefully more than shown here, but this does demonstrate the ability to keep the wheels driving on the ground even over rough terrain, spreading the load and maintaining momentum. The low and rather neat-looking tailgate can be seen in the upright position here, and the two curved bars that supported the sideframe assembly of painted wood.

The usual five dials were mounted on their own plate in front of the driver. At the bottom of the photo is the steering column, with the locking lever on the left in the unlocked position so that the column can be telescoped down. Note how the three pedals are relatively close together, grouped around the steering column. To the right of the instruments you can see the black circular control for adjusting the electric trailer braking system. The Warner system could be adjusted depending on load, with the dial going from Light to Heavy balance.

Although there was a canvas cover for the front driving compartment, there appears to have been no consideration given to protecting the soldiers in the rear beyond the wooden slatted sides – such as you'd find in a vehicle transporting livestock. This may well have had something to do with the need to keep a low silhouette, and it's obvious in this shot how long and low the vehicle is if you take down the canvas top and lift out the wooden rear section. Note also the central pivot of the two rear axles visible between the rear wheels. Ground clearance was 8.75ins and height 56ins.

The data plates show that this was MT-TUG 11, and was delivered on 20 May 1943. Only about another four were ever built. Note that the maximum speed was still posted as 55mph, although it seems unlikely that, especially laden, the vehicle could have managed that speed.

WARTIME JEEPS

An unusual arrangement for the levers. At the top is the handbrake on the left, with, in the centre, the lever for the front axle lock and, on the right, the lever for the two-speed transfer case. On its own at the bottom of the photo is the normal gearlever for the three-speed plus reverse gearbox, albeit remotely operated from this rearward position. Leather gaiters were used because of the scarcity and expense of rubber.

Close up of the steering box under the wing on the driver's side. Not a great place, as it would be in the path of mud and muck coming up into the wing. Just below it can just be seen the exhaust pipe on its way to the other side, as it exited in front of the rear pairs of wheels.

WILLYS MT-TUG

The neat tailgate is now in the down position ready for getting troops or kit in and out. The rear lights have rubber seals although these would probably not have made it through to full production. Above the taillight this side is the sprung cover for the electrics socket for when a trailer was towed. Beneath the tailgate in the middle is the pintle hook ready for the trailer.

Either side at the rear were two cargo boxes. On a normal Jeep they would be accessed from the top, but on this vehicle they were accessed from the outside. On the exterior of each was a reflector, and the stowage lids were hinged at the top with a simple catch at the bottom. Note also the metal bracket support on the right for the wooden upright.

99

WARTIME JEEPS

The two rear axles are clearly visible here, with the front one somewhere in the distance. They are Spicer Model 23, fully floating axles with a Spicer Model 25 at the front. Note how the rearmost differential unit is offset to the left, allowing the two propshafts to come down the vehicle side by side. The propshafts were attached at the front to the Spicer Model 186 transfer case. This unusually had three outputs, two for the propshafts to the rear and also one on the top for a possible power take-off. In the foreground either side are the Houdaille shock absorbers – they were mounted either end of the dual leaf spring set-up and you can see their large mounting brackets attached to the chassis. These were adjustable for ride control, with a locknut being eased off to allow adjustment via a screw to offer softer or firmer ride. It's doubtful if this would have been used much under normal conditions, even with varying loads. As you can see, this is a complicated, heavy, power-sapping arrangement all round.

The common suspension support between the rear two pairs of wheels. The standard combat split rims carry 6.00x16in tyres. No spare tyre wheel and tyre was carried so one can only assume that it was felt that the 6x6 would be able to get out of trouble even if one wheel was punctured or destroyed.

WILLYS MT-TUG

The Go-Devil L-head engine in yet another engine bay. The MT-TUG's main mechanical changes aren't visible here, and include a Warner T84J gearbox and Spicer 186 transfer case. Given the added weight and complexity of the vehicle it was now being asked to power, it's doubtful the engine would have been powerful enough in the reality of combat operations. As with all these Jeeps photographed here, the single 12-volt battery would have originally been two six-volt batteries.

It's a Jeep! The Jeep logo cast into the cylinder head between the spark plugs.

Chapter 10
WILLYS T-28 Half-Track

The Jeep was the original go-anywhere vehicle, but for some that just wasn't far enough. America's most westerly part, to the west of Alaska, was the chain of islands that make up the Aleutian Islands. Remote, often covered in snow and mostly made up of extinct volcanoes, the islands were, even so, militarily significant during the war.

Aircraft were frequently travelling from their build home in California to Russia as part of the war effort and their stopping-off point was the Aleutian Islands. The islands gained further importance when the Japanese actually invaded and captured two of the islands in 1942 in an unsuccessful attempt to deflect the Americans from the critically important Battle of Midway.

Moving around the snow-covered lava fields and hills of the islands was virtually impossible for most vehicles, and the military began to worry about defending this approach to Alaska as well as about rescuing airmen if their aircraft went down on any of the atolls.

Since even a Jeep wouldn't be able to manage it, efforts were made to produce a vehicle with the ability to carry people and with a significantly lower ground pressure per square inch. The first prototype, the T-29, was based on the 6x6 TUG Jeep – see previous chapter. It had a half-track rear and skis instead of the front wheels. It was found to be difficult to steer, didn't carry enough and was also too hard on the tracks, which wore quickly.

Since it was Willys-Overland who had created the T-29, it was they who were tasked with finding a more practical solution. But all of this took time. It was late 1943 before the design became to be built up and it was August 1944 before the first of three T-28s was delivered to the US Army at the Aberdeen Proving Ground for testing.

The Half-Track Litter Carrier Snow-Tractor T-28 was its snappy title. It's not surprising that it soon became known affectionately as the Penguin Jeep. As you can see from the photos, it's a larger vehicle than a normal Jeep and certainly seemed to tick all the boxes at first. It had a ground pressure of less than 2psi, a remarkable figure for such a large vehicle, and perfect for staying on, rather than breaking through, snow and ice crusts. It could carry two stretchers, one above the other, on the passenger side, and there was seating for three people facing inwards behind the driver. It certainly looked like it could fulfil the requirements of heading out into the snowy wastes and picking up downed airmen, injured or not.

The whole vehicle was longer, wider and taller than a standard Jeep. This was accomplished by cutting and extending the original Willys chassis. With the extra size and weight, the Go-Devil engine was breathed on to increase power to 63bhp at 3900rpm. Three versions were built and, depending on the version, there was drive only to the rear or also to the front wheels. If the front axle was powered then the standard 6.00x16in tyres were replaced with larger 7.50x16in tyres. There was still the facility to replace these wheels and tyres with skis if the snow was very thick and powdery.

At the rear there was the obvious change to the tracked assembly. In a tank the wheels are all metal and use metal teeth to engage with the tracks. In the Penguin Jeep the rear axle was fitted with two metal spoked wheels with special tyres which had heavy cleats to grip the track. In front there were two bogie wheels either side, again shod with rubber tyres. Although it looks a strange set-up there seems to be no loss of traction by the rubber tyres on the track.

The track itself was a composite arrangement made of rubber with metal inserts. The experience of the T-29 showed that track wear could be a problem, but the much stronger arrangement on the T-28 showed no signs of early ageing.

WILLYS T-28 HALF-TRACK

Clearly some thought had gone into this vehicle, even though it was a prototype. The extensive use of chequerplate, not only in the rear compartment, but also for areas like the step area into the front seats, showed that it was anticipated the Penguin Jeep would be used in harsh conditions where ice and snow would make moving around difficult. Even so, the prospect of being injured, lying on the top stretcher in the rear, with only a flapping layer of canvas between you and the ice and snow would be enough to freeze anyone's blood.

Despite all the positive attributes of the T-28, which was given extensive testing time, the end result was a thumbs down. By this time it was April 1945 and the war was clearly nearing its end. After 698 miles of testing, the Army just didn't feel this was a vehicle they wanted to put into production. The main reason given was that the steering was solely by the front wheels. Even though the track assembly worked well, there was no way to steer with the tracks and this fact alone was enough to stop the programme from ever going live.

Although it never made it into full production, the Penguin Jeep shows just what a versatile, rugged vehicle the original Jeep was, and just how many different uses it could be put to.

Classic Willys front end, but it's rather different behind the windscreen.

WARTIME JEEPS

Given the harsh environment in which the T-28 was designed to operate, the very least the soldiers could hope for would be a complete set of canvas. And the very least is what they got.

The V-shapes in the bodywork were to strengthen the structure as the vehicle could have been carrying as many as seven men across extreme terrain. The rear spoked wheel is from the Ford Model A car. You can just see that the rear axle has its own leaf springs, with the hangers visible either side of the rear wheel, while the two bogie wheels shared a leaf spring, visible between the two wheels.

WILLYS T-28 HALF-TRACK

Details of the track assembly, inside and out. The rubber tracks had metal cross-pieces bolted into place and then the metal sections were themselves infilled with further rubber sections.

WARTIME JEEPS

The wide tracks were one of the main improvements over the T-29. In fact the T-28 had a ground pressure of less than 2psi, which kept it from sinking through snow and ice crusts. There were two rear doors. The one on the right allowed easy access to slide a stretcher in and out of the vehicle

WILLYS T-28 HALF-TRACK

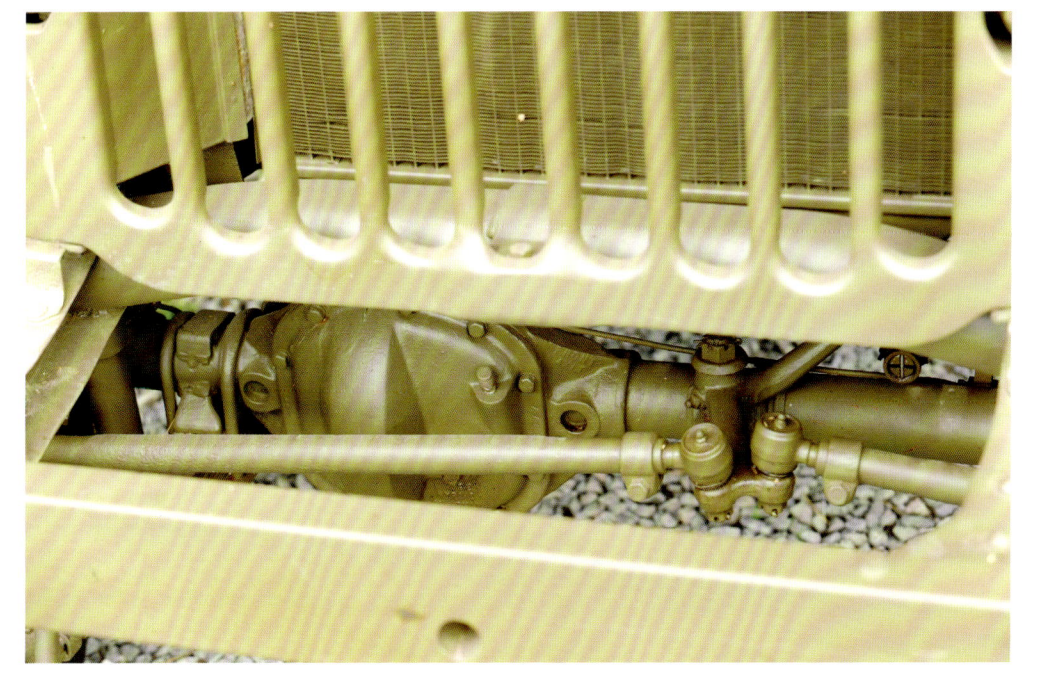

The Penguin Jeep is remarkable to drive. Although there's a fair amount of clonking and rattling, as you'd imagine, it actually drives very well and the lack of track steering does not seem to be a major problem – although it's fair to say we were not using it in an extreme environment. This shot clearly shows the lash in the tracks, but the very high mudguard leaves plenty of room for track movement as well as for clods of earth and snow to go through without jamming up the tracks. The transfer case had to be revised to take into account the different ratios in the rear axle and also the different radii of the front and rear wheels.

Front axle sits just under the curved, tubular framed Willys front crossmember.

107

WARTIME JEEPS

Note the chequerboard plate at the top, above the chassis crossmembers. Excellent shot showing how the tyres and tracks integrated. The original cleated tyres are long gone, but these more normal tyres still work well under most conditions and provide plenty of traction to the tracks. The exhaust is not original and is made of stainless steel to the original mild steel design. To the right of the silencer box you can see the propshaft running back to the axle down the right hand side of the vehicle.

The T-28 was unusual in many ways, and one of them was that the fuel tank was for once not placed under the driver, but where the passenger seat would have been. The simple flap covering the filler has been opened, showing the felt seal in place.

WILLYS T-28 HALF-TRACK

The wood and metal slats provide the framework for the canvas cover, which surely would hardly ever have been taken off in operational use. On the right the two stretchers are held securely by metal frames. Note that they extend into what would have been the passenger seat. This had to be removed to make way, with the extra seat moving to the back, inside the rear door. On the left are the three squab seats which could be for wounded personnel or else medical crew. Even though the vehicle was designed for extreme weather conditions, the driver still only got a manual windscreen wiper, with a connecting rod so that both wipers worked together.

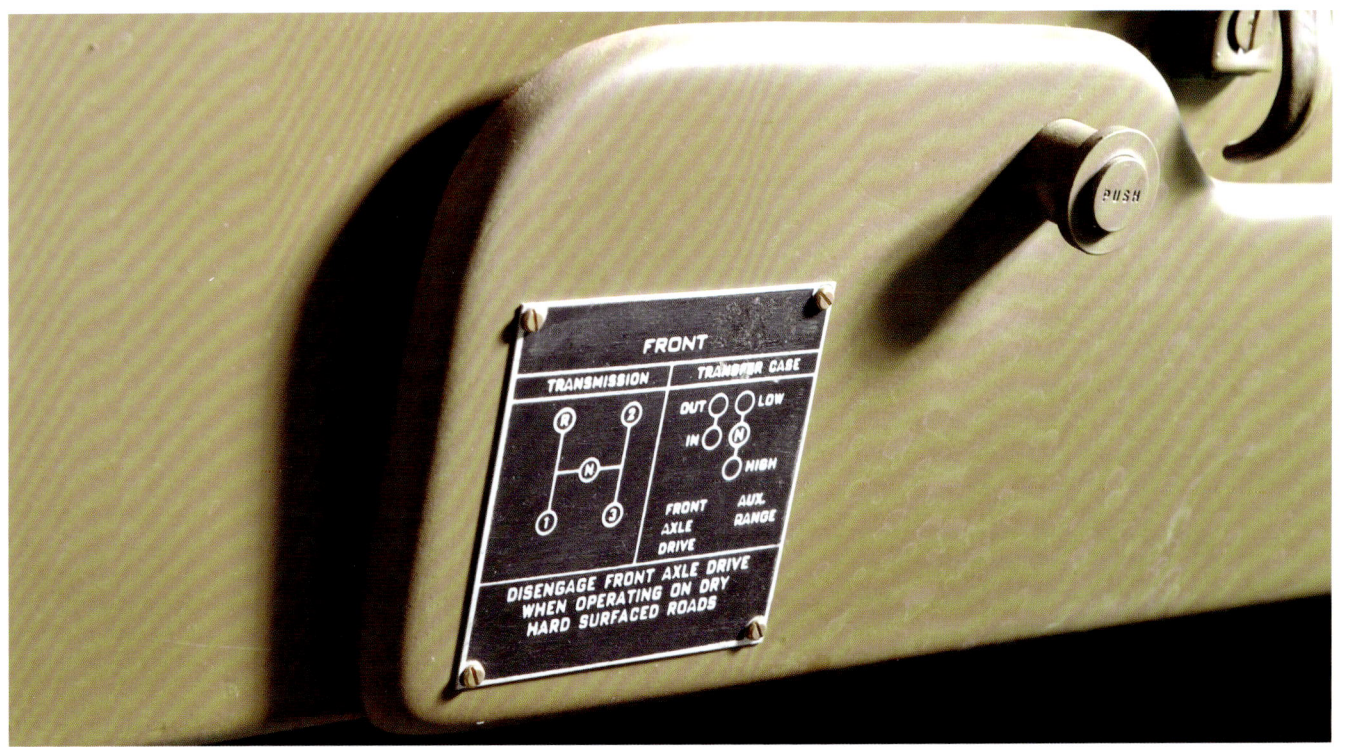

Compared to the GPA, the T-28 is a model of restraint when it comes to giving information. This later-type glovebox has a simple push button to release it instead of the locking type.

WARTIME JEEPS

More normal looking cockpit, featuring all the standard dials and the later composite green steering wheel. Note how the carrier poles of the stretcher jut forward into the cabin, leading to the removal of the passenger seat.

That'll be the original speedo then. It shows that this particular vehicle has only covered 946 miles in its long life, and the majority of those were clocked up in a brutal series of tests by the US Army in 1944 and 1945.

The shared leaf spring suspension of the two smaller bogie wheels each side. The shape of the track blocks can clearly be seen here, showing how much grip they could exert.

WILLYS T-28 HALF-TRACK

Once again, the Go-Devil finds a new home. In this case a slightly more spacious home. This is an easy bay to work in. Note the air cleaner (back left) leading to the carburettor (right) sitting above the manifold. The distributor, in front and right of the air cleaner, is also high up and easily accessible.

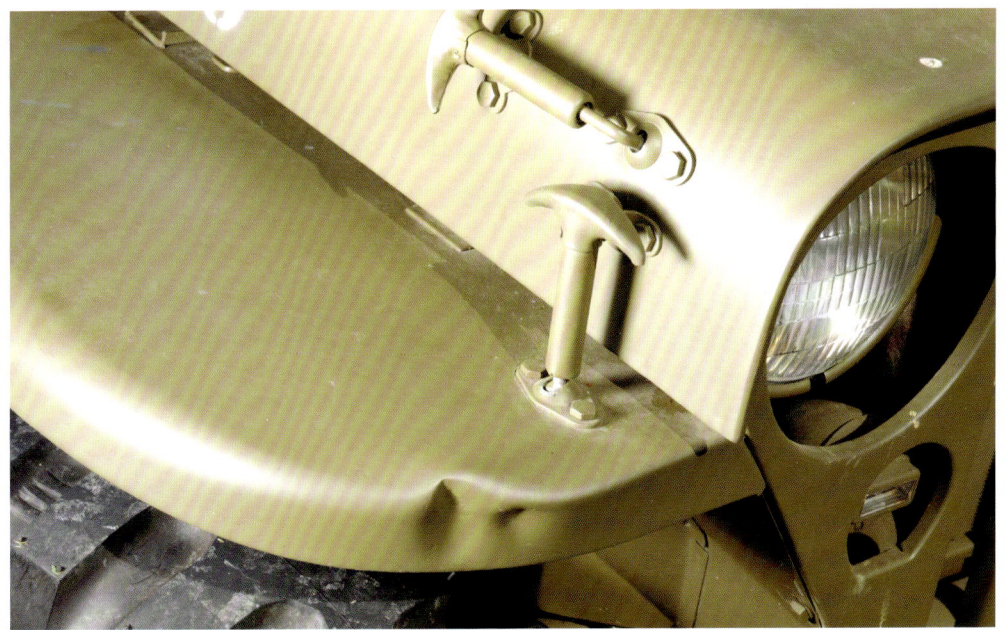

"Number 39" is one of the more famous Jeeps as it was photographed during and after the war. In 1944 it was photographed without a rather famous ding in the front wing, but by 1949 there it was. And here it still is. The rest of the vehicle was restored but this original dent is still in place.

111

Chapter 11
SAS WILLYS MB

The Special Air Service was conceived in the deserts of North Africa in 1941. Here they worked with the Long Range Desert Group (see Chapter 6) but, once they'd helped win the desert campaign, they were transferred to Europe and played their part in the brutal fighting of 1944 and 1945. Amid the mud and flood of the winter of 1944, some of the same men who had fought in the harsh heat of the Sahara continued their work of reconnaissance and combat. And they used the same vehicles.

By this stage the SAS, formed into the SAS Brigade, were being used for parachuting in behind enemy lines, doing deep reconnaissance and generally living on the very edge of combat as the Allied armies ground their way through Belgium, the Netherlands and then into Germany.

In the great sand seas of the Sahara the SAS, unlike the LRDG, had operated with the Jeeps being almost totally self-contained. Photos show them laden with jerry cans of fuel and water. Ironically, now that they were in Europe, they found they still needed to be totally self reliant. When you're probing into remote villages, unsure if the Germans are still in the area, miles ahead of your troops, you can't count on having any kind of back up at all.

The Afrika Korps was a formidable enemy but in Europe the SAS might suddenly come upon a Waffen SS battle-group, with battle-hardened soldiers heavily armed with the latest weapons, who were now fighting to keep the enemy from their own country.

In this incredibly hostile environment, the mavericks of the SAS had to look after themselves. Which they did. They took their trusty Jeeps, sprayed over the desert colours with dark green, stripped even more bits off and then added even more fuel, armour and armaments.

One such result is this 1944 Willys MB, which is an exact copy of a vehicle crewed by Sergeant Schofield and Trooper Jeavons. They were with B Squadron, 1st SAS Regiment, and in late 1944 were tasked with deep reconnaissance for the First Canadian Army.

The very first thing you notice of course is the firepower. This Jeep has five Vickers K guns. Each gun has a magazine holding 100 rounds and the high rate of fire means all of those bullets could pour into a target in just six seconds. If both driver and passenger were firing their front guns that gives 300 big .303-calibre rounds into a target in six seconds of concentrated fire. In terms of destroying a target, that's job done, but the other aspect was that they were equally useful at firing at enemy aircraft and at the important job of keeping the enemy's head down while the driver got the Jeep turned round and out of range as soon as a

The real thing. Trooper Jeavons is driving, with Sergeant Schofield manning the guns. They were with B Squadron, 1st SAS Regiment, which was part of the SAS Brigade in Northern Europe in 1944-45. This chapter explains why they are aren't smiling, but instead are looking pale but determined.

contact had been made.

The guns were originally designed and used on aircraft, and aircraft further provided some of the added protection. Both driver and passenger had armoured glass added in front of them, although it's not clear exactly what aircraft it came from. It's two inches thick and would have been reassuring when the bullets started to fly. In front of the driver this glass is attached to a large armoured plate. The passenger's twin guns were mounted on a swivel pintle with the armoured glass and plate also attached so they swivelled with the guns, offering more protection as the guns traversed. A searchlight was attached to the front of the plate, with another mounted on the bonnet. You'd have to be brave to think you saw something in the gloom and then switch on the searchlights – but, then, they were brave.

Bearing in mind that reconnaissance was a primary aim, the twin guns in the rear would have provided ample covering fire for when the vehicle needed to get away with information gleaned. Another steel plate is bolted to the rear panel to provide extra protection, with extra magazine drums clipped to the inside of it for easy access.

At this stage of the war, enemy aircraft weren't a major problem most of the time, but clearly any Messerschmitt going in for a strafing run would find itself facing an off-putting amount of fire coming up from a very small target.

From the crew's perspective, perhaps the most worrying aspect was the addition of two large fuel tanks sitting up fairly high behind the driver. A tap in the fuel lines could bring them in once the main tank under the driver's seat was empty, but it must have been a source of worry under fire, just as much as a reassurance that the crew wouldn't become stranded through lack of fuel.

To compensate for the extra armour plate and weapons, just about everything else has been stripped off the Jeep. You can see the number of holes in the bodywork where nuts and bolts have been removed to take off everything from the grab handles to a spade. Weight burns fuel and is liable to bog you down, so this Jeep is about as light as it can be while laden with lethal munitions.

The crew needed to be fairly nimble, after all they weren't a tank and had other duties to perform. The classic example is what Sergeant Schofield and Trooper Jeavons had been doing just before that famous photo of them was taken.

Trooper Jeavons was the driver and Sergeant Schofield was manning the guns as they probed along the border of the Netherlands and Germany, ranging ahead of the First Canadian Army. At some point, despite being told not to, they crossed over into Germany and came into a village to see who was home. The German army was. As they came up a lane into the village they realised the troops milling around ahead of them didn't look terribly pleased to see them. Things took a turn for the worse when they found further up the lane that they were looking at the back end of a Panzer. The tank began to traverse its turret round towards them as it sought to bring its 75mm cannon to bear on their Jeep.

Time to leave. While Schofield gave covering and suppressing fire, which kept the enemy's heads down but which didn't bother the tank, Jeavons had to perform a three-point turn in the narrow lane, all the while watching the gun coming round. At this point how they must have wished that the four-wheel steer version had gone into production.

Once facing away, they floored it down the lane and managed to scoot into cover just before the tank's gun could get them in its sights. They headed back to their unit and were stopped on the way to have the photo taken (see opposite page). All things considered, they look remarkably calm, if a little pale.

As an aside, it is believed that Trooper Jeavons was killed soon afterwards but Joe Schofield, although wounded in action in 1945, survived the war and stayed in 22 SAS until the 1970s. The SAS Brigade lost around 330 men killed or wounded between D-Day and VE-Day. In that time the 2000 men in the Brigade inflicted around 7733 casualties on the enemy and took nearly 23,000 prisoners.

Against a backdrop that camouflages the vehicle and the crews' clothing, the most stand-out item is the famous red beret with SAS badge. Guns to the front, guns to the side, guns to the rear – so many guns, so many targets. However, trying to steer with your right hand and aim and fire the machine gun with your left hand while working the pedals must have been a co-ordination nightmare for someone under the stress of combat.

WARTIME JEEPS

Front view is almost entirely taken up with lights, guns and armour. The armour plate is quarter of an inch thick in front of both drivers and the armoured glass is two inches thick. The effect is only slightly ruined by realising that the box in front of the driver's armour is actually full of ammunition. Although the passenger here is standing fairly tall, it's obvious that if both crouched down the crew would be fully behind extra protection in the event of a firefight. At least until they had to turn round.

As a consequence of stripping stuff down but then adding more, in this case the kit on the passenger wing and the machine gun pintle on the driver's side, it was felt necessary to add the extra support struts from the wings down to the shortened front bumper.

This shot clearly shows the extent to which the SAS went to reduce weight to allow them to carry more precious firepower, armour and fuel. All the holes in the side of the Jeep result from taking off, among other things, the windscreen, wing mirrors, axe, spade, grab handles, canvas roof supports and bits of wing. If it rained they got wet and cold. They didn't need to see what was behind them. And if they got really stuck then there would be no friendly helping hands to join in dragging the Jeep out of a ditch.

Note also the reinforcing for the pintle for the Vickers K gun beside the driver and also the way the rear extra armour plate is stepped to cleanly attach to the rear of the Jeep.

SAS WILLYS MB

The armament made this Jeep all but a flying fortress, ready to fire on targets on the ground or in the air. The Vickers K guns were sometimes known in Britain as the VGO gun, Vickers Gas Operated gun. Originally they went back decades, and were found on aircraft like the Fairey Swordfish, but as planes, particularly bombers, moved over to belt-fed multiple machine guns in turrets, a lot of these Vickers K guns were left looking for a home. The fledgling special forces, such as the SAS and LRDG, made good use of them.

WARTIME JEEPS

In this shot it's easier to see how the front mudguard has been cut off just aft of the pintle mount for the machine gun. Below it can be seen the extra torque reaction spring kit added to the driver's side to help with braking in a straight line. This vehicle is not carrying a full fuel load so those extra tanks are now empty, which would make a big difference to the weight. However, it must be noted that even with all the armour and weapons the Jeep is sitting fairly flat and the springs aren't under intolerable load.

That extra armour plate, a quarter of an inch thick, would come into its own when the crew needed to get away. Note standard spare wheel attached in a new position, right on the outside of the driver's side, so as to allow room for the machine gun pintle in the centre. The wheel is held by the standard three-bolt holder. It not only provides a chance to keep going in the event of a puncture or shredded wheel, it also offers some protection to the large fuel tank behind it. On the other side that task is taken up by a box for spares. Note the unusual placement of the shovel, held by the rear towhook and a canvas strap attached to the rear crossmember. This would have held the two bumperettes – but they too have been removed.

SAS WILLYS MB

On a cold, snowy day in the winter of 1944 this must have been a difficult vehicle to drive, let alone do dangerous reconnaissance work in or get involved in a firefight. Good shot of the thick, heavily braced pintle for the machine gun on the driver's side, and a clear view of how the passenger could swivel not only the machine guns but also the armour and searchlight which were attached. The round magazines could hold either 60 or 100 rounds.

The driver's position shows that the weight-loss programme continued inside. Switches and dials that would serve no purpose are missing. Even the data plates have been removed from the glovebox lid to lose a few ounces. Note the height of the protection in front of the driver, although he could hinge down the armoured glass part when not heading into trouble. The shot also shows the passenger's machine gun pintle coming down through the bonnet in front of the bulkhead before being bolted to the floor. Given the recoil from two .303 machine guns, the pintle needed this level of support. This Jeep has a quick-release boss for the steering wheel so this may have been originally used by airborne or special forces. Although it is a replica, the original 1944 Willys MB base vehicle appeared to have many of the SAS tweaks already done to it, so it is guessed that the base vehicle actually was an SAS vehicle, if not this exact one.

WARTIME JEEPS

The Simms spotlight in the centre of the bonnet was in a fixed position, while the other one swivelled with the armour plate it was attached to.

Although it wasn't strictly necessary in the cooler climate of Western Europe, the removal of most of the bars from the front grille quickly became a bit of an SAS trademark. This did leave the radiator open to damage but it doesn't seem to have caused many problems in practice. However, the condenser tank which often went with this modification really wasn't necessary and, for the sake of weight and simplicity, was not added.
Note that the front bumper has been cut down, again for weight, and also something of an airborne-forces tweak. The bumper carries the two lifting rings so that in theory the Jeep could have been swiftly moved for transport and then dropped behind enemy lines. However, it's noticeable that the two rings that you'd expect to find at the rear, behind where the bumperettes would have been, are not fitted.
Passenger wing carries a first-aid kit held in a custom metal frame. Night blackout headlights have been removed, and there is extra strengthening to the bumper and mudguards.

SAS WILLYS MB

Spare magazines are held on the inside of the armour plate. Some of the vehicles had a mix of weapons – Vickers Ks, Bren guns, even .50 cals – but in this vehicle there was no need of mixed ammunition. These drums fed everything. Note the fillers and feeds for the twin fuel tanks and, between them, discarded packs and Thompson sub-machine gun.

Detail shot showing how the armoured glass was held in place within the clamped and bolted metal frame. Again, you can see – note the number of holes. The extra fuel tanks were held in place by two metal straps which hooked over and through eyes welded on the top of the bodywork either side.

Appendix
JEEP SPECIFICATIONS

Chassis
Separate ladder-frame chassis with steel body panels. Box-section steel side-rails with five cross-members

Body
Floorpan in 16-gauge low-carbon steel. Body panels in 18-gauge low-carbon steel. Panels attached through 16 bolt holes with fabric shimming

Length overall
132.2ins

Width
57ins (62ins including handles)

Height
40ins (top of bonnet); 69.7ins (top of canvas roof)

Wheelbase
80ins

Wheel track
49ins

Ground clearance
8.7ins (axles); 10.1in (bodywork)

Fording depth
21ins

Weights
2450lbs unladen
Maximum payload: 800lbs
Maximum trailer load: 1000lbs

Approach angle
45 degrees

Departure angle
35 degrees

Suspension
Spring steel semi-elliptic leaf springs. Eight at the front, nine at the rear with telescopic dampers. Dual-spring torque-reaction mechanism under driver's side front springs

Brakes
Twin-shoe drum brakes, hydraulically operated to all wheels

Wheels and tyres
Split-rim 16in combat rims. Tyres 6.00 x 16 NDT (Non Directional Tread) with inner tubes. Tyre pressure: 35psi

Fuel
15 US gallons capacity. Range of 116 miles at 50mph (218 miles at 35mph)

Engine
Go-Devil in-line water-cooled four-cylinder
Displacement: 134cu ins (2199cc)
Bore x stroke: 79.4 x 111.1mm
Valves: L-Head design, ie inlet and exhaust valves located in the cast-iron block instead of in the cylinder head. Valves parallel to the cylinders
Camshaft: Single camshaft, chain driven
Compression ratio: 6.48:1
Clutch: Single-plate, dry
Air cleaner: Oil-bath type with oil capacity of 1 pint (0.47 litres)
Carburettor: Single-barrel downdraught with throttle-operated accelerator pump
Power: 55bhp at 3600rpm/60bhp at 4000rpm
Torque: 105ft lbs at 2000rpm
Liquid-cooling capacity: 11 quarts (10.4 litres)
Oil capacity: 5 quarts (4.7 litres)

Transmission
Three-speed, plus reverse, synchromesh on second and third. Type Warner T-84J

Transfer case
Two-speed. Type Dana Spicer 18

Axles
Spicer Dana 4.88:1. Front: Dana 25. Rear: Dana 23-2

Electrics
Six-volt electrics (negative ground) with 40-amp QMC generator
Distributor: Camshaft-driven with full automatic advance
Headlights: Sealed beam 45w

(Specification is for a bulk run vehicle, either Ford GPW or Willys MB. Operational necessities caused changes to weight and specification over the long production run.)

Production figures
Bantam BRC-40	2572
Willys MA	1500
Willys MB	335,531
Ford GP	3700
Ford GPW	277,896
GPA	12,774